The Art
of the
Compliment

A Man's Guide to a Relationship

Jonathan Clyde Moore

Published by

Suck Free Publishing

Copyright Notice

Library of Congress Cataloging-in-Publication Data

Moore, Jonathan Clyde, b 1961

      The Art of the Compliment: A Man's Guide to Relationships/ Jonathan Clyde Moore

ISBN - 978-0615438702

First Edition – January 2011

Dedication

Are all my books really dedicated to my father? So far; yes. He taught me nearly everything I needed to know and though he is not perfect, he is a good man and I strive every day to live up to the ideas he taught me to hold. And although I share a lot of qualities with my father we also have some fundamental differences. But even while growing up he never disparaged me for these differences, he just insisted I pursue them with integrity and resolve, no matter that he thought I might be making the biggest mistake of my life. And at times he did.

What better gift can a father give to his son?

So, thank you Dad, for being there, for teaching me what it means to be a man, and for everything. That I have a great relationship with my sons is due to the foundation you gave me.

However, I do have two additional dedications. Since 2008 I have been a member of Neopoet.com, an on-line writing workshop. A number of the folks at Neopoet.com have worked with me in specific workshops and other events and their feedback has helped me improve the style and quality of my writing and I am grateful for their advice and support. And lastly, to all the folks who chose, over the last three or four years, to seek me out and ask my advice on relationships, the opposite sex, and your family, the hope and promise you had and the confidence you showed me was inspiration to create the Compliment form of poetry and in October of 2010 to start a 14 day writing project that became this book.

It's like serendipity because, well, it was serendipitous.

Other Works by Jonathan Clyde Moore

Suck Free Poetry Volume 1: Flatearthers and Other Dreams

Suck Free Poetry Volume 2: Prelude to a Battle of Wits

Suck Free Poetry Volume 3: A Question of Caricature

The Map Story and Other Tales – March 2011

All titles are available at the following locations:

CreateSpace.com

Amazon.com

SuckFreePublishing.com

Bookstores and Online Resellers upon request

Table Of Contents

Introduction

First things first; guys, you may have gotten this book as a gift which is a direct violation of the whole concept of gifts covered in a later chapter appropriately entitled Gifts and Holidays. Do not, under any circumstances, throw this in her face when you read that chapter. Trust me on this because of all the good decisions you will have made in your life, it most definitely would not be one of them. Man up, move forward.

Now; let's get on with the show.

Why did I write this book?

Did I write it to help men get in touch with their feminine side?

Hell no.

Admit it guys, if we ever got in touch with our feminine side we'd never leave the house.

I did not write this book to help you get in touch you're YOUR feminine side, I wrote it to help you get in touch with HER feminine side.

Because, and let's be truthful, everything we do has a motivation of seeing her naked. It's OK to admit that, she already knows it; we just have to be smarter about the whole process.

So let's get started, shall we?

There are those who might question a book of relationship advice written by someone who has been twice divorced, hell, I certainly would. I won't bother giving excuses, I'll just ask you to take a look, see if anything I say seems worthwhile, and give a try to whatever sounds good.

But let's set some expectations right off. This is not a book about how to get the girl. It's not a book on how to make her love you. This is a book for those guys who know they've got a good relationship and want to remind themselves and their girl of it.

This is a book for men who are not afraid to tell their loves that they know full well how lucky they are. This is a book for the man who may not always have the words or ideas or inspiration to demonstrate how they feel. But most importantly, this book is for the man fortunate enough to be with that person for whom they would gladly do stupid things.

But we won't be doing stupid things because, gentlemen, that does not actually impress the ladies, it just makes them grimace and love you in spite of yourself. And what we want is for them to love us because of who we are and what we do and for this, well, this book will give you some tools.

There is a caution, however. This book is not merely a relationship guide. It contains observations and strategies for men to employ that show the women we love that we know we could do no better and neither can they.

That's right guys. It's OK to admit you are the brass ring, you are the prize in the box, and you are the best thing that's happened to her. Because you've already admitted she is the best thing to happen to you and we are not going to be begging and whining and pleading for her to notice us. We are not 12 years old. We are grown men of ability and knowledge and we need to learn how to treat her in the female equivalent of how we want to be treated.

Because, gentlemen, the clear and honest truth is that women are not like us. They respond to different things, they like a different focus, and they are as alien a creature to which most of us will ever be hopelessly attracted.

I'm not judging here, just stating facts.

And the facts can be summed up in this saying.

Men are children, women are insane.

And that is not an insult; it is a statement from each perspective. Women look at us and say, "What children." And it is true, we men like childish pursuits. The issue is that most of us readily admit it and even revel in it.

And when men look at woman and their actions we think, "Damn, they are insane," because, from our perspective, they are. And that's the hurdle we have to get over. Women have already mostly reconciled themselves with the fact that we will always act like children. But we have not reconciled ourselves with their behavior and we are puzzled and perplexed by their actions and end up getting upset and angered when they act as their nature dictates.

The base problem is not that women are insane; the base problem is that we keep choosing an incompatible brand of crazy.

So this is the first and most important lesson, choose a crazy you can love and embrace. Tolerating her brand of crazy is not enough. She deserves better than that and so do you or it will end messily.

After all, if you meet the perfect woman for someone else, you'll just end up being the idiot who lost Sandra Bullock because you did not choose the right type of insane to fit your life. And really, no matter who comes into your life next, how the hell do you explain losing Sandra Bullock?

So don't be that guy, chose a brand of crazy that's compatible with your own because the basic fact is that everyone is impossible to live with and any excuses you make now will turn into resentment later and the stupid things you choose to do will not be the kind of stupid things that add to a relationship.

The Only Rule

It pains me that I even have to write this down.

No hitting.

And please, spare me the "what if?" crap scenarios. We both know we are talking about everyday life, not during a self-defense class, not fooling around or accidents, not weapon related situations, and not any other "aliens and the end of the world" stories some males make up because they want an excuse.

A real man does not hit a woman.

Ever.

A real man does not hit a woman back.

Ever.

A real man walks away if things have disintegrated to the point where he is being hit by the woman in his life. Walk away, get calm, and let her get calm.

It's not because we are generally stronger. It's not because we pretend to be more logical or reasonable. It's not because we are taking the moral high road or embracing the lessons of non-violence.

It's because it is wrong.

I was 16 years old the last time I ever joked about the subject of striking a girl. I was relaying a story about my job to my dad and thoughtlessly slipped in a comment akin to "the next time she does this I swear I will hit her." My dad stopped me and explained in no uncertain terms the same thing I have stated above.

A real man never hits a woman. Ever. A coward might. A 12 year old boy might, not one of his sons but a 12 year old boy raised by a father who was a moron, perhaps. But a real man never hits a woman.

If you want to argue about this, find a brick and strike it against your head until you believe everyone thinks you are pretty because this is one of the few rules I will state categorically. If you are male and you believe it is OK to strike a woman, you are a coward and a fraud and when real men find out what you are doing they will explain to you the error of your ways in terms that will take three to six weeks to heal.

If you are lucky.

If you are so angry you cannot think straight, walk away. I've been there, I've been on the receiving end of fists and plates and accusations and threats.

Walk away.

The only thing worse than enduring the above actions is trying to explain to your friends, family, police, and the guy in the cell next to you what you have done; so walk away. It's better to have a "crazy woman" than a "lonesome Bubba" story to tell your friends over a beer.

The rest of the book is filled with suggestions and strategies and all of it should be taken and applied as best fits your life but this is the only rule and I will repeat it because it is critically important.

No hitting.

I am convinced that if I were to ever attempt to hit a woman that my mother would rise from the grave and my father would hold me while she slapped me.

And I would deserve it.

My parents taught me better than to hit women. If there has been a failing in your upbringing and you have not had this explained to you yet, I am explaining it now and you no longer have any excuse, ever, to hit a woman.

I could make some useless threat at this point but it will have no effect on the stupid and if you are so stupid you think it is acceptable to strike women, I just hope your life does not include procreation.

Be a man, don't hit women.

Getting Started

There are some very important things we need to understand as we approach this guide. If you forget these items, all you are doing is ensuring you and whoever you are with will be unhappy.

- Jealousy is not cute, it's insecurity
- No one deserves to be treated badly
- Making excuses for her behavior is building resentment
- If you have to change her to be the person you want, she is not the person you want
- There are important things, there are unimportant things, choose carefully
- Realistic standards are not too high
- If you believe you are "settling" you don't deserve her
- Everything you tell your friends and family will get back to her, say it to her first
- All these items apply to her too

It's really quite simple. There is no secret, there are no rules, and any 10 step list is a waste of time. There is only the connection. If you have a connection between you both, you can build on it. If there is no connection, all you are doing is marking time until you part company.

So man up and own that connection. The worst thing that will happen is that you will make a fool of yourself. Guys, it's what's happening already but right now you are just blindly stumbling around hoping someone won't cheat on you before you leave them.

Really, that's just sad.

If you're not in a serious relationship, fine, make certain you both know that. If you think your relationship is or is getting serious, are you planning for the future or are you waiting for the break-up?

Three Things

We're guys. We like simple things. This is simple.

There are three things you need to keep in mind about women:

- They like to be noticed
- They like to be appreciated
- They like to be pampered

So, what should you do? It's simple:

- Notice her
- Appreciate her
- Pamper her

"WHOA!" I can hear you now, "Pamper her? I let her get me a beer, that's not enough?"

No. And you don't let her get you a beer; she decides getting a beer for you makes her feel good because of the way you react. She does it because she is letting you know how important you are to her.

"She's saying all that just by getting me a beer?"

Yes. Now, pay attention.

You believe you've found a woman who cares about you, likes you, and realises how great you are; excellent. If you don't demonstrate your awareness of the same things about her, you are an idiot. Remember, while you can't make the wrong woman love you, you can drive away the right woman through your indifference and insecurity.

So man up.

If it helps, think of all of this as foreplay. Trust me, she does. And always remember the test for anytime you think you need to argue. There are important things and there are unimportant things; choose carefully.

Notice Her

Notice her, couldn't be simpler, right?

Apparently it could because we, as men, do not notice her. You can tell by the way her face lights up when other people notice her. Her friends notice her, her co-workers, the waiter, and the clerk behind the counter, and anyone else who goes out of their way to remind themselves to be polite and attentive towards her and is rewarded with that smile.

Hey, you can share that smile with others but why are you allowing others to share it with you? Whenever she receives a compliment the first thing in her mind should be, "I love hearing that from strangers too," rather than "why can't he ever say things like that?"

So take 15 minutes out of your day; really look at her when you see her. When something changes, tell her. It might be her hair, shoes, smile, makeup, clothing, or what-ever. The point is, look at her, and I mean really look at her. Notice her like you were going to paint a picture of her from memory.

Think about it for a second. Don't you want her to notice if you've been working out or mowed the lawn or built something or if you just feel particularly good for no reason? She wants the same thing and by taking 15 minutes to notice her, you get a head start on everyone else who sees how wonderful she is and remains certain she can do better than you. Right now she's convinced, against all that is right and good, that you are special in a good way. So take 5 minutes three or so times a day to show her it's true.

Yes, that was math, deal with it.

Appreciate Her

"Appreciate her? She knows how I feel!"

No, she doesn't. We're guys, we solve problems. We don't make a lot of assumptions, we ask questions, we get answers, we make decisions, and we move on. So why the hell should you assume she may know how you feel?

Are you afraid of showing emotion?

Are you afraid your friends will ridicule you?

Are you a 12 year old boy?

Dear God boy, grow a set of balls and man the hell up. Look at her. You care for her; for some yet undetermined reason, she cares for you, why the hell are you being a whiney little boy about this? Tell her you love her. Tell her you appreciate the things she does. Tell her you know how lucky you are.

If your friends give you a hard time about it mention this to her and be prepared for the next goodbye kiss in front of them. Think about it. Your friends are giving you crap about you telling her how much you appreciate and love her. Do you have any idea what this does to a woman? Your friends will, and they will be asking you how you managed it; after all, you only told her you'd see her soon and that you loved her.

The message here is stop worrying about what other people are going to think and start preparing to explain why they are so envious of you. Because it is simple; we, as guys, want to be appreciated. Now we like our appreciation to be a little differently focused but to get that focus we need to appreciate her in the way she wants to be appreciated.

And the best thing about appreciating her and letting her know, it adds around five extra minutes to your day. You're already there, you're already talking, hell, in a lot of cases letting her know you appreciate her will save you time.

Pamper Her

Bad news guys, this does not mean sex.

Sorry, but it's true. Hell, trust me, I am as disappointed as any other guy that our desire to separate them from their clothing is not considered noticing and appreciating and pampering but the reality is that it is not and we are guys, we are supposed to understand the whole reality thing.

And we need to avoid the other end of the spectrum. We need to limit the huge gestures because they are so damn public. When you give a woman a car or a pony or an expensive dinner or whatever, you are not pampering her you are saying "Look what I got with my money!" And hey, if that's the type of woman you want, throw this book away, it's useless to you. If you're looking for the exception rather than the shill, keep reading.

Pampering should be small and private. Don't bring her a dozen roses, bring her a rose. Don't send her flowers, bring them home. Make her a cup of tea or coffee, rub her feet, rub her hands, cook her dinner, remember she really wanted that new whatever and get it for her. Ask her to pick the next movie and enjoy it even if it's only the coffee and dessert after the movie part.

And compliment her.

And I don't mean you should tell her she is pretty. Everyone else is saying that. You want to stand out. You want for her to think every compliment she hears pales in comparison to the ones you give her. You want to show her that you love her, that you desire her, that you admire her so much that it becomes part of your life together.

It's not the power of positive thinking; it's the power of a considered life. And guess what, this takes around 10 minutes a day. We'll cover compliments in detail a bit later. You have some groundwork to do before your compliments can make a difference.

And the rewards? Hell boy, it'll make the "Appreciate Her" moment blush.

What Next?

We've had a bit of introspection. We've had a bit of lecture. I've called you some pretty harsh names and demanded you man up and stop whining and so at this point you'd like me to tell you that you're making progress and will soon be on the path to eternal happiness.

That's not going to happen. And I am not even sorry.

Next comes the hard part. I've detailed three simple things that add around 30 minutes to your day. Truthfully, some days it will be less, some days more but you will need to plan on 30 minutes because we are men and we love to plan things.

Plus, once you plan you have a better chance of doing more than reading this book, thumbing through the pages, and letting it, and your relationship, gather dust.

Anything worth having is worth working for and a relationship is no different. So carve out 30 minutes a day, not all at once, and work. I can hear it now, "What do you mean by 'not all at once?'" Guys, this is not a chore, this is a new hobby. You have to approach this as something you either love to do or care enough about the end results to pretend to love to do.

Over the next chapters we will plan and scheme and bludgeon you into a mindset that will make you happier by reminding yourself how lucky you are. A side effect of this is that she will be happier and more content and, think about it, more attentive.

Now, of course, this is not a guarantee. It is a logical conclusion from available evidence and if the only thing that happens is that you decide the woman is not worth the effort, well, I may have just saved you a car or a house or a lifetime of misery.

You are very welcome.

Attitude Adjustment

That's right; it's time to wake up.

If none of this applies to you, you have my permission to feel smug.

As men we get a lot of conflicting messages as to what it means to be a man. I'm here to tell you to ignore all of it. My dad fathered five boys, was in the Navy for 20+ years, loved and buried one wife and was lucky enough to find another woman to spend his life with. He played sports, coached, fixed everything, and mentored more people than I can remember.

My dad is the best man I know and he taught me the only important thing you need to know about being a man. A real man does whatever is required to get the job done.

That means you can't be afraid to know how to clean or cook or change a diaper or make coffee or put the frigging toilet seat down. If you are running around with a list of things a real man does not do, you are an idiot. You are no longer acting like a child when your responsibilities are done, you are a child and this book may do you no good what-so-ever because it makes the assumption you are not defined by what all the other frightened little boys say or do.

I took the lessons my father taught and the lessons my mother added and I used them hardcore when, at 26, I was the custodial parent of a 10 month old boy. So I cook and clean and change diapers and keep the toilet seat down because you only need to find your toddler playing in the toilet once to end all argument.

Now I've also done martial arts for over 15 years and am a 3rd degree black belt, I break, without spacers, a stack of six 12"x12"x1" boards with my hand, I break a 2" concrete slab with my hand, I do break-falls and tumbling on asphalt, I teach sparring, I throw five punches in a second, I do 50 pushups in 30 seconds, I get a six pound quarterstaff moving so fast you can't see it, I strap on armour and trade hits with a variety of weapons. I officiate at MMA matches and I play nearly any sport competently. I run up stairs. I can build a fire from scratch. I do basic carpentry, plumbing, electrical work, and masonry. I do fire performances and build my own equipment for them. Did I mention I was 50?

So if you want to call me names because I'm not afraid to write or recite the woman I love a poem, go ahead. After all, it's not you I'm trying to convince to shed your clothes.

And that's the attitude adjustment men. Stop worrying about what your incompetent friends will think and start worrying about how you will keep this amazing woman in your life. Because unless you plan to sleep with your male friends and have sex with them, I am missing the point where their approval of your behavior can be of any importance, unless you are just an insecure 12 year old boy waiting to be told what to do by other insecure 12 year old boys.

So be a man because she's ready to be done with boys.

If you do not know how to cook or vacuum or dust or do laundry or dishes or change a diaper or sew on a button, it's time to learn. And what if she doesn't know how to do all the traditionally male stuff? What then?

Who cares? This is about us. Let her worry about her, trust me, you don't want that hassle.

But there is a caveat. What if you go through the book and take it to heart and learn to do it all and implement every part and she doesn't like the way you do all these things? What if she wants you to do them her way?

The answer is "No." Depending on how the question was presented, the answer might very well be "hell no!" In some cases it might even be, "Goodbye."

If you are doing the jobs, it does not matter how your methods might differ from hers. If she has a cheaper or more effective way of doing it, take a look if you want. If she just demands you do it her way, the answer is no.

End of story, case closed, done.

We're here to get things done; she'll need to lighten up. If she can't, well, you have a decision to make as to how miserable you are willing to be in order to have her in your life because you will be miserable and it will not get better.

Let's look at it from another perspective. How long do you want to be around a woman who less and less frequently has worse and worse sex with you and spends her time telling you and others what a horrible person you are just in the hopes that she might one day decide to touch your penis?

There's just not enough pretty to cover that amount of mean.

So let's start by assuming this woman, this person, this amazing girl in your life deserves your best just as you deserve her best and what if you do not know how to cook or clean or anything like that because you've always been a boy and no one taught you how to be a man?

No worries, I am here to help. We'll lay out some basic chores that are required to keep a house in acceptable working order and I'll give you simple instructions on how to accomplish the tasks.

Housework

Housework must be done. You can either spend an hour trying to avoid it, another hour arguing about it, and a lifetime wondering why she left or you can man up and learn what to do. There are six basic jobs involved in housework:

1. Dusting
2. Sweeping
3. Vacuuming
4. Mopping
5. Scrubbing
6. Putting Away Your Crap

It's not that hard and if you do not know how to do housework, it does not make you manly; it just shows you are a little boy with limited skills and less value that will drive everyone but your mother out of your life as you whine that you wanted the RED truck and just 15 more minutes playing Nintendo and EVERYBODY else has got a jean jacket and you'll hold your breath until you turn blue.

Admit it, we know grown men like this. They brag about their exploits and the way they've bent some woman to their will and at one point you've realised it is worse than sad, it is pathetic and they are telling the same stories they did when they were 12. If you're looking for a mommy, change nothing. If you're looking for a woman, man up, be a man.

How? Let's break this down, shall we?

We'll cover how and when to do these six basic chores. These are not complicated instructions gentlemen. They fit on a single page, there is a list, and all the major steps are defined.

Let's get started.

Dusting

Where: baseboards, furniture, frames, windowsills, lamps, racks, corners and nearly anything else that collects dust

What: feather duster, occasionally a rag and polish (furniture polish, glass cleaner, water, as required by the situation. Do not mix these.)

When: Weekly

Length: 10 minutes per room

How:

1. Use feather duster for 95% of all dusting
2. Brush feather duster against everything that has accumulated dust
3. Occasionally clean feather duster by banging it against an outside wall or in a garbage can
4. Items that may need to be polished
    a. Wood
        i. Spray furniture polish on rag
        ii. Wipe down wooden furniture
    b. Electronics
        i. Use a lightly damp cloth sparingly
    c. Everything else
        i. Spray an ammonia based cleaner on a rag
        ii. Wipe down
        iii. Use second rag to wipe dry
5. Replace tools when finished

Notes: Dust first. The will knock dust from items to the floor and when we sweep and vacuum, everything gets taken care of.

Sweeping

Where: Non-carpeted floors

What: Broom, dustpan, garbage can

When: Weekly

Length: 10 minutes per room

How:

1) Retrieve required tools
2) Pull things away from walls
3) Sweep behind things
4) Put things back
5) Sweep rest of room, moving whatever is required
6) Sweep into dust pan
7) Empty into garbage can
8) Replace tools when finished

Notes: Sweeping is just like raking. Hell, there's a thing called a broom rake, it does to your lawn what you should be doing to your house.

Vacuuming

Where: Carpeted Area

What: Vacuum cleaner, extension cord

When: Weekly (more if you have pets that shed)

Length: 10 minutes per room

How:

1. Unless your vacuum can easily reach everywhere you need to clean, plug in an extension cord to save your temper
2. Plug in vacuum
3. Vacuum all carpeted areas
4. If you have a furniture attachment, use it on upholstered furniture
5. Move items as required to vacuum under and behind them
6. Replace tools when finished

Notes: Vacuuming is a hassle and I do not like to do it. I would like it less if I had to change bags so I got a bag-less model vacuum. I highly recommend it. An upright will be easier to manage and mostly cheaper even though a canister model is more versatile.

Never, never, never buy her a vacuum as a gift. Buy her flowers, and buy the vacuum as a tool you both need. Trust me on this. I was never stupid enough to do this because my mother and father taught me right from stupid. I've seen it happen, it's never pretty.

Scrubbing

Where: Counters, porcelain, metal, appliances

What: Scrub pad, soapy water, bucket, if desired

When: Weekly

Length: 10 minutes per kitchen and bathroom

How:

1) Put 4 squirts of dishwashing soap in a bucket or sink
2) Fill with hot water
3) Dip scrub pad
4) Wring
5) Scrub ALL areas, not just the ones that look dirty
6) Change water if it gets too cool or too dirty
7) Empty and rinse sink/bucket and scrub pad
8) Replace tools when finished

Notes: Wiping is not scrubbing. Wiping is something you do a few times a week. Scrubbing is what you do before company comes over and when you forget about it for a few months this 10 minutes becomes an hour at a time you can least afford.

So scrub weekly and save yourself the hassle and embarrassment of the results of not scrubbing.

Mopping

Where: Non-carpeted floors

What: Sponge mop, soapy water, bucket (if desired) floor polish (if desired)

When: Weekly

Length: 10 minutes per room

How:

1) Put 3 squirts of soap in sink or bucket

    a.   Use special floor soap if you want to feel special

2) Fill with water

3) Put mop in water

4) Remove from water and wring over bucket or sink

5) Mop floor space, moving things as required

6) Rinse mop often in soapy water

7) OPTIONAL: Using floor polish

    a.   Put down floor polish appropriate to surface, following directions

    b.   Use clean mop to polish floors

8) Empty and rinse sink/bucket and mop

9) Replace tools when finished

Notes: I use a sponge mop because it's easy; you can use anything you want, including your hands and knees and rags, I really don't care but you need to mop because it removes those random sticky spots on the floor and picks up what sweeping misses which is never as visible as when it is most inconveniently seen by guests or company or her or worse, her parents.

Putting Away Your Crap

Where: The whole bloody house

What: Your two hands

When: Daily, at least

Length: Less time than required to argue about it and end up sleeping on the couch

How:

1) Be a man, clean up after yourself

2) If you take it out, put it away

3) If you unfold it, fold it

4) If you get it dirty, wash it

5) If you empty it, throw it away, replace it with a spare, and put it on a shopping list

6) If you are the last person out of the bed, make it

7) And remember

    a. If there's not a full serving left in a container, it's empty

    b. If there's not enough toilet paper left on the roll for you, it's empty

    c. If you would be annoyed if you went to use it, man up and fix it

Notes: By doing these six things, call it three hours each week, you are already ahead of the game. You've just saved yourself at least one fight a week of no less than 30 minutes. You've just saved yourself one fight a month no less than two hours. You've just earned yourself a special spot the next time she gets together with her girlfriends and they all complain about the men in their life and subsequently tell her she should keep you around because you are a find.

That's right, the dreaded girlfriends will be doing the job of selling you to her and it will only cost you a few hours a week of crap you should already be doing.

The Other Four Things

So, are you ready for more? Of course you are. This stuff isn't all that hard, it's just annoying to remember to do. That's why I construct a calendar of chores, print it out, and post it on the fridge to document all I am doing. It is a subtle reminder to anyone who stops by what a great person I am because the assumption will be I am the typical boy-child who needs his nose wiped. But one look at the list and suddenly I am the exception.

And the good news is that there are only four other major chores rounding out housework. The bad news is these can be more complicated so may span more than a single page.

1) Grocery shopping
2) Laundry
3) Washing dishes
4) Cooking

I know some of you are freaking out about now. Grab a beer, take a deep breath, and brace yourself. Boys are taken care of by their mommies, men take care of themselves. If your mommy still cooks for you and does your laundry and all the food shopping and the only thing you know about washing dishes is that it a woman's job, you are a pathetic moron destined to wonder why men you consider to be wimps get the girl of your dreams and why the woman you are with is a soul-sucking harpy.

It's because they are men and they've attracted all the woman and you are left with the girls with unresolved father issues who resent you more and more each day and are planning to leave you as soon as the right person comes along which, coincidently, is the same thing you are planning.

Hell sucks.

Grocery Shopping

Grocery shopping should always be done with four things

1) Menu
2) List
3) Budget
4) Calculator

The menu does not need to be complex. You'll need a main, side, and desert for each day. And don't get stuck on traditional diets, just focus on things you like and will eat. This will both save arguments over what to have and arguments over wasted money when things are thrown away.

Later on in the cooking section we'll cover some simple and quick recipes that have a low per serving cost and are delicious. But it starts with a menu and that menu can be as simple as:

- Monday – Spicy baked chicken, salad/vegetable, fruit (yes, fruit can be a desert, live and learn)
- Tuesday – Sautéed beef and vegetable, pie
- Wednesday – Boneless pork chops, salad/vegetable, ice cream
- Thursday – Omelet, warm cheese Danish/ fruit tart
- Friday – Pan seared chicken and fresh greens, pie (you have it left over from Tuesday!)
- Saturday – Seasoned steak and mostly mashed potatoes, ice cream
- Sunday – Homemade pasta sauce, salad, warm cheese Danish/ fruit tart (you have it left over from Thursday!)

So what happens if you or she is a vegetarian? Substitute eggs, meat substitutes, nuts, eggplant, etc.

And what if you are a vegan? You are on your own.

But, now that we have a menu, we can make a list to match the menu. And since you've already put down anything you've used and need like milk and butter and salt and the like, we don't have to worry about panic or impulse buying.

So you've got your list and you've got you menu and you damn well better know your budget, so take your calculator and go to the store with your girl.

Why? There are three main reasons.

1) You're an idiot if you think it's a woman's job to shop

2) She'll know you think her time is valuable

3) You'll understand the price of food better

At this point someone will mention coupons and I admit it, I don't do coupons. If your mate wants to do them, let her. Don't ridicule, don't harass, and don't meddle. Just let her and the coupon thing go and move on.

Whatever your budget is, understand you'll go over at times but try to keep it at no more than 10%. That's what the calculator is for. Also, since you know your menu for the week, if you can buy a larger amount for a savings, do so, bring it home, segment it into servings and store or freeze the parts you will not be using immediately.

There are a few side notes of grocery items.

- Store brands are normally comparable quality and cheaper
- Sometimes the store brand is a waste of money – learn and make note
- Look for the discount spices, they're fine for our needs
- Frozen vegetables are more versatile than canned
- Boneless meat has less waste but costs more
- When in doubt, check the per ounce cost

Notes: If at all possible, count on shopping two or three times a week for groceries. This reduces impulse buying and gives you a better idea of when a special is a waste of time and money. It also means you spend less time each trip in the grocery store. Say 20 minutes a pop rather than an hour. Yes it averages out to the same but admit it guys, we start to get annoyed after more than 30 minutes.

Laundry and Sewing

First, if the label says DRY CLEAN ONLY, don't argue about it; just take it to the cleaners. Next I've got some good news and some bad news. The bad news guys, is that no one likes doing your laundry. The good news is that it ain't that hard to do.

Laundry is a five step process.

1) Separate your clothes

2) Wash your clothes

3) Dry your clothes

4) Fold your clothes

5) Put away your clothes

And that's it. Of course Steps 1 and 2 have some tricks to them so we'll break these out.

We won't be separating by color. This is why you should only do your laundry and not hers. She'll get upset when you mix her reds with her whites. Also, if you make a mistake and wash your shirt on heavy, it'll be fine. If you wash her delicate items on heavy, you'll shred them and she will not be happy, no matter what your intent.

I get it; this is scary for you, this is why I've got a chart; so calm down and take a gander. This is easier than you think and most of your clothes will fall into five main categories, each with a water temperature and cycle that is appropriate.

Load	What goes in this load	Water Temp	Wash Cycle
1	Socks, underwear, and undershirts	Warm	Normal
2	Work clothing (yard, car, sport, etc.)	Warm	Heavy
3	Towels and bedding	Warm	Normal
4	Casual shirts, pants, and sweaters	Cold	Perm Press
5	Jeans, fleece, and like items	Cold	Normal

I'll be honest; I wash almost exclusively in cold. It's cheaper and since I wash my clothes regularly, does a great job. Some people insist on washing things in hot water and that's fine but you need to remember, we are cleaning clothing; we are not disinfecting it to sterile hospital standards.

But what about drying? Easy, dry everything on medium heat unless the labels states otherwise. Always check the label; it's easier, and cheaper, than replacing it.

There are a few exceptions to the washing rules but they are simple. For new clothes, I wash them by color in cold and on the permanent press cycle to set the dye. You only have to forget to do this once before you realise it's a gamble you do not want to lose.

For dress shirts, I recommend you take them to the cleaners. It's cheap and they do a better job of ironing than you will. If you feel you must do it yourself, wash them with your casual shirts and dry them normally.

As far as ironing, keep the following three things in mind

1. Check the clothing labels and chose the correct temperature setting for the fabric
2. Once you put the iron to the fabric, NEVER stop moving it
3. Use spray starch

If I have to go over how to fold and put away your clothes, we have a bigger problem, so I am going to hope against hope you know how to fold your own damn things. The reasons you want to fold your clothes is so they look like they belong to a man, not a 12 year old boy, when you wear them. The reason you want to put away your clothes is because then you know where they are and never ask the innocent question:

"Have you seen my green shirt?"

Because that seemingly simple question translates to the following thought-chain for the woman in your life:

1) I can't believe he can't do his own laundry

2) What does he think I am; his maid?

3) Does he expect me to do everything for him?

4) "Frank" does his own laundry (this may be a friend or an ex)

5) Will he ever grow up?

6) I used to think this was cute

7) If I asked him where something was he'd ridicule me!

8) Why can't he get a better job!

9) I hate him!

And seriously guys, it's your own damn clothes. Man the hell up and learn how to take care of them your own damn self.

Notes: If your washer has a lint trap, find it and empty it before every load. Your dryer has a lint trap, do the same thing, find it and empty it before every load. This saves time and money and means she'll never have to wonder why you can't do something as simple as empty the lint trap. See the above though-chain for an idea of what goes through her head when you never empty the lint trap in the dryer.

Basic Sewing Repair

Gentlemen, sewing takes practice but there are things you can do to not appear like such a lost little boy.

Frist, buy an inexpensive sewing kit. It will have needles and thread and thimbles and pins and some crap scissors. Next, buy a small box, put the sewing kit in your car for emergencies, and duplicate everything in the sewing kit in your box. This will expand to include the following:

- A pack of hand sewing needles
- A pack of straight pins
- A needle/pin cushion (think small stuffed toy)
- A couple of thimbles
- 2 pair of inexpensive scissors (general office supply scissors)
- 2 measuring tapes
- White, black, blue, brown, and tan thread, to start

And that will do for now. Next, let's cover how to do some basic repairs. We'll cover rips and holes and seams and buttons since they are the most common issues.

General Notes:

If these are work clothes, just concentrate on making them not look like you are homeless. If they are casual clothes, take more care. If they are business casual, determine if it is worth fixing or is it better to replace it, and if it is formal, take it to a professional.

Threading a Needle

I'll give you the way I use, not necessarily the professional way because I'm not a tailor, just a guy who can do basic repairs to his own clothes. If someone else tells you a better way, use it.

- Cut length of thread a little more than twice as long as you need
- Put one end of thread through the needle hole
- Fold thread in half, tie loose ends together
- Move needle to middle of thread
- Done

The First Stitch and the Last Stitch

Again, this is what I do. It's quick, easy, and has not failed me in 40 years. If someone tells you a better way, embrace it. The first and last stitch anchors the repair, so we want to make certain they do not pull through the material.

- Always start your first and last stitch on the back or hidden area of the item, it looks better.

- Push needle through the target area, leaving about 1" of thread behind

- Make your stitch length no more than 1/8", smaller is better but takes longer. Larger not only looks bad but will part and fail

- When needle is back through to the start side of the stitch, pass it through the loop of thread you left when you started and pull tight

- Continue stitching with either 1/8" vertical (zig zag) stitches separated by 1/8" gap or horizontal (double) stitches that create a solid line of thread along the repair area. To help you out, there are illustrations below

Stitch Illustrations

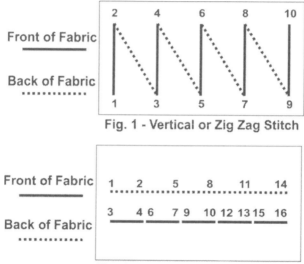

Fig. 1 - Vertical or Zig Zag Stitch

Fig. 2 - Horizontal or Double Stitch (these are separated into two lines for illustration purposes only, the stitches should overlap)

Rips

Rips can be from stress or sharp objects or any other number of things and when they happen at a non-seamed area will always leave a scar on the garment so be prepared for it and make your decision before you start if it is worth repairing.

- Trim ripped area to remove frayed threads
- Turn garment inside –out

- Pin ripped area together with a 1/4" overlap
- Sew using short, even stitches below the pinned area
- Sew both ends of the rip twice as these are the weakest points
- Remove pins

Holes

Holes are bigger than rips and usually indicate there is significant material missing. For holes you will need a patch. A patch can be a similar material, which is great, or something to make do in an emergency, which is fine as well. If you decide on an iron on patch, realise you are infusing glue into the fabric so any sewn repair will be problematic. Most holes will come at knees and elbows, just like when you actually were a 12 year old boy.

- Determine location of patch, internal or external
  - An internal patch is not as visible as an external patch as it only shows through at the hole but the frayed area remains visible
  - An external patch is very visible but can look deliberate, especially if you match it with an identical patch in a symmetrical location.
- Cut patch for area
- Pin patch to garment with pins close to patch edge
- Stitch around the pins if using a zig-zag stitch or directly under them if using a double stitch
- Remove pins

Split Seams and Hems

Seams and hems are a special case. With each, the stitches have failed and you need to repair them. The first thing you need to do is review the type of hem or seam. Is it just two pieces of fabric pressed together with frayed edges protruding or is the fabric folded over and then pressed together, thus matching the frayed edges of each piece and leaving a clean seam? Whatever the case, you want to duplicate it.

You also want to duplicate the stitch used if at all possible. Other than that, follow the same steps as you would for a rip.

Buttons

Most of your button issues will be with button down shirts. Occasionally you will have an issue with a coat, but we can use the same principles there.

Buttons are easier than you think. The first thing to do is to make certain you have a button that is identical or nearly identical. The original button is always preferable but, in a pinch, there are options.

If you cannot find the original button or one that looks like it, look at the cuffs of the garment. Notice those extra buttons on a shirt and the extra buttons on a coat? Great, Remove one from each side. Now you have a replacement button and a spare and the garment does not look horrible.

Let's get started then:

- Look at how the button is attached, just to get an idea
- Clean the button location of excess thread
- Sew on the button crossing diagonally in front, horizontally on back
- Make certain the button has enough "play" or separation from the shirt to be useful
- When you are satisfied that your button looks similar enough to the other buttons, wind thread around the thread under the button as if you were wrapping a cord
- Tie off the wrap
- Finish with final stitch to back of garment

Sewing Machines

None of this requires a sewing machine. Though fixing hems and seams is easier on a machine, you can get by without one. As such you do not need a sewing machine but if you feel like experimenting, go for a basic model so that when it sits and collects dust you don't feel as stupid as you did when you had to have that new tool or piece of exercise equipment still sitting in a closet, in its original packaging, unused.

Washing Dishes

Of all the household chores, washing dishes is probably the easiest to screw up. If you vacuum before you dust, no worries, at least you did both. If you wash your casual shirts on heavy, you'll get over it. If you go to the grocery store without a list or budget, things will work out. But when you screw up the dishes you scream to your woman that you don't know anything.

The reason is simple. There is more to washing the dishes than washing the dishes. See, it's cryptic, so it's no wonder you screw it up. Not to worry, we'll get through it.

Washing dishes does not have to be difficult; all you need to do is follow a plan. Hey, we'll be fine; we get to make a plan. The first part of our plan is to ask her to dry the dishes. Trust me on this.

When you ask her to dry the dishes you are telling her that you want to spend time with her in a non-sexual manner and that you will do the tough part of the job. Even if you cooked, you still want to be the one washing the dishes.

Why? Because you control how long you are in the kitchen and you get to touch her every time you want to hand her something. A small caress as you are passing her a dish or a glass or a pan will set a mood.

Remember, everything we are doing has a direct result and an indirect result. The direct result is that the things get done and you fight less. The indirect result is that everything you do becomes foreplay because you are telling her that she is important and worthwhile and that you plan to stay around and that you like spending time with her even when her clothes are on. And caressing her hand with a finger as you pass her a dish does not hurt.

Fine, but what about the dishes?

Firstly, if you have a dishwasher, use it for the basics but save some things for the actual dishwashing experience like pots and pans and other items that are cumbersome. With the dishwasher, be the one to load it and empty it. Also, spare her ire and rinse the plates. Modern dishwashers do not require it but really, do you want to argue about this? Remember the simple test for an argument; there are important things and there are unimportant things; choose carefully.

As far as the non-dishwasher items or if there is no dishwasher, I've got you covered. Just follow the plan below.

1) Scrape plates, empty glasses, put way any food (and package her lunch for the next day)

2) Put several inches of hot tap water in pans and set aside

3) Fill sink/basin with hot tap water and 3-4 squirts of dishwashing liquid

4) Organize items

    a. Glasses and cups

    b. Plates, bowls, and platters

    c. Flatware and utensils

    d. Anything else

5) Wash each category of item and hand it to her with the occasional caress or put in the drainer if you were too stupid to get her involved.

6) If the water looks dirty, it is, empty it and refill

7) Wash pans, scrub as required

8) If the water looks dirty, it is, empty and refill

9) Wipe down all appliances

10) Wipe down all counters, moving things to get behind and under them

11) Rinse sponge, dishcloth, etc.

12) Empty sink/basin

13) Rinse sink/basin

14) Give her a hug and a kiss on the cheek or neck

15) If she wants a kiss on the lips, do not be surprised, indulge her

Notes: Do not neglect changing the water when it gets dirty. It only takes a couple of minutes and you can fill that time by giving her a hug and asking her about her day. You can even listen for a change.

Cooking and the Kitchen

This chapter is about cooking, not baking. I will admit it, I do not bake. Not only do I not bake, I steadfastly refuse to follow the directions correctly to succeed at baking. I view cooking as art to which we apply science. I view baking as science to which you apply art. So if you can bake and do not want to do the cooking, that is fine and good. If you neither bake nor cook, you are the problem. If neither of you bake, no worries, buy. Remember, there are important things and there are unimportant things, choose carefully.

For some reason cooking scares folks. They think it has to be grand or expensive or take a lot of time or be incredibly messy or expensive and I suppose it can be for some folks but I'm giving you 10 recipes, most of which cook in around 30 minutes for a per serving cost of $3 or less. What's more, my recipes normally make four servings so you can take leftovers for lunch, plan a leftover night for your menu, and pack her a lunch and have all her friends be envious of one more thing about you while they favorably compare you to their mates and once again do the job of selling you to her.

There are three important rules to cooking:

1. Make certain you have the ingredients you need
2. Make certain you have the equipment you need
3. Thaw frozen meat in a bowl for two (2) days in the refrigerator

The first two are common sense and so are often forgotten or overlooked. The last one is critical because all the preparation in the world will not solve the problem of a frozen piece of meat when you need to cook dinner and there is almost nothing worse than the blood from meat running unimpeded over your refrigerator shelves and dripping down onto everything. If it sounds disgusting it is because it is disgusting. So use a bowl when thawing meat and thaw it in the fridge because it is safer and less problematic. I have not been pleased with the results of thawing in the microwave, so I do not.

What if you don't have kitchen equipment? If you do not have kitchen equipment, it's time to get some. Here are the basics of what you will need:

- Pot and pan set (start small, a 10 piece set, including lids, you can add later)
- Cookie sheet (general use item for heating rolls and breads and the like)
- Oven roasting pan
- Knives (full tang, otherwise you will throw them away quickly)
- Measuring spoons, measuring cups
- Cutting board (2)
- Vegetable peeler
- Grater/slicer (I use mine rarely but they are cheap and a good option)
- Can opener
- Corkscrew
- Colander
- Whisks(s), spatula(s), large spoon(s), often sold in sets
- Mixing bowls (these double as storage and serving bowls)
- Apple corer
- Melon baller
- Timer
- Spices (salt, pepper, basil, oregano, sage, cinnamon, garlic, ginger, onion powder, cayenne pepper, and more if you want)
- Dish drainer
- Sponges, dish towels, dish rags, 2 each
- Flatware, cups, glasses, and place settings for four (more if you'd like)
- Food storage containers (I recommend getting just one size, that way you never have to hunt for a lid to match and they can become your lunch container for leftovers.)

As you put together your kitchen supplies you will need to make decisions about quality and price. My preference is to spend money where it does the most good. I buy heavier and more durable pans and knives, cheap as possible measuring spoons and cups, whisks, peelers, etc., and a basic timer. I will admit the collapsible colander stores easier and that sold me on it.

A general rule for pots and pans and knives, weight matters. Better quality pots and pans will be heaver because the metal will be a better gauge and it will have a heavier bottom. A heavier bottom generally means more even conduction of heat which translates into fewer hotspots in the pan and a more predictable cooking environment. This is a good thing.

For knives, a full tang knife will be heavier and will take an edge better and will be more resistant to bending. I generally go with a knife set rather than individual knives and although will have one or two of the "never needs sharpening" knives on-hand, I like the traditional knives for their handling characteristics and feel. If you do not care about this, no worries; go with what you like.

You may wonder why there are two cutting boards. They are inexpensive and having a spare is great when you have to cut up meat and anything else at the same time. You never want to use the same cutting board for other things as you do for meat without washing it first. In some circumstances you will be short on time, so having a second cutting board simplifies the issue.

We are not pretending to be gourmet chefs, so start with the less expensive spices. If you get to the point where you know the difference between types of cinnamon, upgrade your spice selection as desired. Until then, let's start with the basics and save some money. Yes, fresh spices are always better than dried spices. Dried spices last for a much longer time.

Lastly guys, when cooking, wash your hands often. Wash everything else too, but start with the hands. Everyone will appreciate it.

As for the basic kitchen equipment you will need, you can spend thousands and buy all sorts of gadgets and jewel encrusted utensils, but I'd recommend keeping it as inexpensive as possible to get things started. Not included in the mix are a teapot, microwave, toaster, toaster oven, a coffee maker, and a range of other appliances. Some people can't live without them, some people can. Make your decision and go with it, remembering that added features mean added money and nothing is sadder than a barista quality cappuccino machine gathering dust when you can't even make your woman an omelet.

10 Recipes

Just a general note before we start. Rinse all food stuffs before using. Not only will it impress her, it removes dust and other things from the surface. And while you are at it, wash your hands often. I've mentioned this before because it is important. Washing your hands prevents cross contamination of foods and while you may think "it all gets cooked anyway" we are normally not cooking vegetables to the same temperature as meat since crisp vegetables taste better. This is a reason we use two cutting boards and two knives. You are welcome to wash them instead of using two but the general rule is "no mixing raw meat and vegetables before they hit the pan."

It's a good rule; follow it unless the recipe tells you differently.

Also, you may notice that apples tend to brown if left too long once sliced. A small amount of lemon juice will prevent this. I put some in a bowl and add my apple slices to it before setting them aside. Try it; see if it's worth the effort.

And then there is clean-up. I normally clean as I go. I keep a sink full of hot, soapy water and wash or rinse things as I finish using them. This fills the time in between cooking steps and leaves a cleaner kitchen when the meal is done. Never underestimate the effect of a fully prepared meal and nearly no dirty dishes on a woman. Just remember all the stereotypical representations of men in the kitchen and be the exception.

Most of the recipes I list are for the main course only. Add a vegetable of your choice to them and while fresh is always preferable, I keep frozen vegetables because of their convenience. Another option is salad and I admit, after years of disparaging it, I use bagged salad. Yes it is more expensive than a head of iceberg lettuce and a carrot and some cabbage and what-not. But I rarely buy the iceberg lettuce bagged salad, preferring the healthier and tastier romaine mix and I can get at least 4 servings out of a bag while it is still fresh. I have less success with individual salad ingredients and normally end up throwing things away which offends both my Scottish nature and budget.

You should make your own choices. Experiment a bit, see what works, what does not, and go from there. And the same thing applies to the recipes; feel free to add and subtract things. I do all the time and some of my best creations have come from just such substitutions made from laziness or necessity depending on my mood and motivation.

A note about my recipes and a reason I do not do well at baking. I don't actually measure a lot of things. All my measurements are approximations because I normally pour or sprinkle from the container. Since you may not be comfortable with this, I am including measurements with the above caveat of, experiment. If you want more or less of or hate an ingredient, what's the worst that can happen? You make a bad dinner, laugh about it and make her an omelet.

And don't even tell me you don't know how to make an omelet. Fine, we'll start with omelets.

Omelet

This is for a single omelet for her. If you want one, you have to do this twice because food presentation is important and you don't want to make an omelet and cut it in half since it will look like you were too lazy to take 15 minutes to make her a special omelet. It looks that way because it is that way.

- Equipment:
  - 1 large frying pan
  - 1 small mixing bowl
  - 2 cutting boards
  - 2 knives
  - Measuring spoons
  - Measuring cups
  - 1 spatula
  - 1 whisk/fork
- Ingredients
  - 3 eggs
  - 1 tablespoon of olive oil
  - 1 tablespoon of diced/shredded cheese she likes
  - 1/8 teaspoon of pepper
  - 1/8 teaspoon of salt
  - 1/8 teaspoon garlic
  - 1/2 teaspoon of basil
  - 2 tablespoons of milk
  - Optional
    - 1 tablespoon of onions
    - 1 tablespoon of a green veg she likes
    - 1 tablespoon of fresh tomatoes, diced
    - 1 tablespoon of precooked meat
- Preparation
  - Put pan on burner at medium heat
  - Add olive oil
  - Set cheese aside
  - In mixing bowl combine all other standard ingredients, use fork or whisk to smooth out
  - Turn pan heat to med-high
  - Pour contents of mixing bowl into pan
  - Chop any optional ingredients, watching pan for thickening of eggs

- o Test edge of omelet with spatula. When you can lift the edge, add cheese and optional ingredients to one half of the omelet
- o Use spatula to fold omelet in half, covering cheese and any optional ingredients.
- o When the whole omelet has thickened and can be easily moved without falling apart, slide from pan to plate
- o Serve

Honeyed Chicken

This is an approximately 30 minute meal and uses a single pan. It's a great last minute thing to cook and is delicious and looks as if it took a lot longer than it did. If it includes something you do not like, take it out. If it does not include something you like, add it. This is not baking, we can play around a bit without having an epic fail.

- Equipment
  - 1 large frying pan
  - 2 cutting boards
  - 2 knives
  - 1 spoon
  - Measuring spoons
  - Measuring cups
  - Apple corer
  - Melon scoop
  - 3 Small bowls
- Ingredients
  - 2 boneless, skinless chicken breasts (or 4 boneless, skinless chicken thighs)
  - 1 medium onion
  - 2 medium carrots
  - 2 stalks celery
  - 2 apples
  - 1 pear
  - 1/4 teaspoon of pepper
  - 1/4 teaspoon of salt
  - 1 teaspoon garlic
  - 1 teaspoon of basil
  - 1/4 teaspoon of ginger
  - 1/2 teaspoon cinnamon
  - 3 tablespoons olive oil
  - 2 tablespoons honey
  - 1/4 cup of cashews or mixed nuts
  - 1 cup mushrooms (or small can, if you do not have fresh)
- Preparation
  - Put pan on burner at medium heat
  - Add olive oil to pan
  - Slice chicken into 2"x1/2" pieces (approximate)
  - Turn heat to medium high, place chicken in pan
  - Add spices to pan

- o Slice carrots, place in bowl 1, add nuts to bowl
- o If using canned mushrooms, add to this bowl
- o Turn chicken
- o Slice celery, place in bowl 2
- o Turn chicken
- o Slice onion, place in bowl 2
- o Turn chicken
- o Slice mushrooms, add to bowl 2 (if using fresh)
- o Turn chicken
- o Core apples, then slice each section lengthways, put in bowl 3
- o Turn chicken
- o Trim pear, slice in half, using the melon baller scoop out seeds, remove stem trail, slice each half lengthwise into 6-8 pieces, place in bowl 3
- o Turn chicken
- o Place contents of bowl 1 in pan
- o Cook 3 - 5 minutes, stirring or tossing pan occasionally
- o Place contents of bowl 2 in pan
- o Cook 3 - 5 minutes, stirring or tossing pan occasionally
- o Place contents of bowl 3 in pan
- o Cook 3 - 5 minutes, stirring or tossing pan occasionally
- o Drizzle honey over pan contents
- o Stir or toss pan 2-3 times to mix
- o Remove from heat
- o Serve

Boneless Pork Chops

This is a very quick meal; serve with a vegetable or salad and bread to complete it. An important thing to remember, if your pork chops are more than 2" thick, cut them in half. We do this for both portion control and for cooking time. Pork is not one of the meats we want to serve rare through intention or neglect.

- Equipment
    - 2 cutting boards
    - 1 large frying pan
    - 2 knives
    - Measuring spoons
    - Measuring cups
- Ingredients
    - 4 - 6 Boneless pork chops
    - 1/4 teaspoon sage
    - 1/2 teaspoon basil
    - 1/4 teaspoon salt
    - 1/4 teaspoon pepper
    - 1/2 teaspoon garlic
    - 1/4 teaspoon ginger
    - 1/4 teaspoon cinnamon
    - 1 medium onion
    - 4 - 6 pineapple rings (canned or fresh)
    - 3 tablespoons olive oil
    - 1/2 cup of soy sauce
- Preparation
    - Put pan on burner at medium-high heat
    - Add olive oil
    - Add spices
    - Add pork chops
    - Slice onions into as many slices as there are pork chops
    - Turn pork chops
    - Add soy sauce
    - Reduce heat to medium
    - Add pineapple juice if available
    - Turn pork chops every 3 minutes (3 times total)
    - Clean up work space while pork chops are cooking
        - Fill sink with water
        - Add soap
        - Wash utensils, cutting board, etc.

- Wipe down counters
- Prep plates, glasses and flatware
- Place onion slice and pineapple ring on each pork chop
- Cook 5 - 8 minutes, stirring or tossing pan occasionally
- Remove salad fixings from fridge, make her salad if you are smart enough to know how she likes it
  - If you are not smart enough, ask, then make it
- Remove from heat
- Serve

Spicy Baked Chicken

If you do not like spicy food, refrain from using the cayenne pepper. Other than this, all spices should be fine. This is a drop dead simple menu item, and tastes like fired chicken without the guilt. Serve with a salad or vegetable.

This is one of the recipes that will take longer than 30 minutes to cook but it is also one of the most idiot proof and simplest recipes in the book. Not only that, but this becomes a great cold snack and can be adapted, with just cutting the pieces smaller, for nugget sized finger food for parties.

- Equipment
    - 1 oven safe pan
    - Aluminum foil
    - 1 mixing bowl
    - 1 cutting board
    - Measuring spoons
    - Measuring cups
    - 1 knife
- Ingredients
    - 2 – 4 boneless, skinless chicken breasts, halved (4 – 8 boneless, skinless chicken thighs if desired)
    - 3 cups corn meal
    - 1/2 teaspoon salt
    - 1/2 teaspoon pepper
    - 1 teaspoon basil
    - 1/2 teaspoon oregano
    - 1 teaspoon garlic
    - 1 teaspoon onion powder
    - 1/2 teaspoon ginger
    - 1/2 teaspoon cinnamon
    - 1 teaspoon cayenne pepper
- Preparation
    - Pre-heat oven to 375 F
    - Mix corn meal and all spices in mixing bowl
    - Line pan with aluminum foil
    - Wash chicken with cold water
    - Slice chicken breasts in half lengthwise
    - One at a time place chicken breasts into bowl, coat with corn meal mix
    - Place on foiled pan

- o Place in oven for 1 hour
- o Clean workspace
- o Stage plates, glasses, etc.
- o Remove from oven
- o Serve

Sausage and Apples

When choosing your sausage for this, make certain it is something you both like. A general rule is that you can add spice to a portion, but not take it away and thus your best bet is to start with sweet or mild Italian sausage. You will want to avoid pre-cooked sausage as it will not taste near as good and its flavor is mostly set. We want the sausage to take on characteristics of our ingredients, thus setting it apart.

Serve with a salad and hearty bread to complete.

- Equipment
    - 1 large frying pan
    - 2 cutting boards
    - 2 small bowls
    - 2 knives
    - Apple corer
- Ingredients
    - 4 - 6" sausages
    - 2 medium onions
    - 2 medium apples
    - 1 teaspoon garlic
    - 1 tablespoon basil
    - 1/2 teaspoon salt
    - 1/4 teaspoon black pepper
    - 2 tablespoons olive oil
    - 1/2 cup soy sauce
- Preparation
    - Put pan on burner at medium heat
    - Slice sausage into 1" pieces
    - Add olive oil to pan
    - Add spices
    - Turn heat to medium high
    - Add sausage pieces
    - Slice onions
    - Place in bowl 1
    - Turn sausage pieces
    - Add soy sauce to pan
    - Core apples
    - Slice apple pieces once lengthwise
    - Place in bowl 2
    - Turn sausage pieces

- o Check sausage pieces
  - They should be just slightly pink in center
  - Continue cooking as required
- o Add onions
- o Cook 3 - 5 minutes, stirring or tossing pan occasionally
- o Add apples
- o Cook 3 - 5 minutes, stirring or tossing pan occasionally
- o Remove from heat
- o Serve

Sautéed Beef and Vegetables

Depending on the cut of beef you get, this recipe may take more than 30 minutes. The better the cut of beef, the more tender it will be and coincidently, the less cooking time required. The cheaper the cut of beef the tougher it will be but there is a solution to a tough cut of beef; cook it at a low temperature for a longer time. This is important, a low temperature. For a stove top, the low setting will be just above simmer or 2 on the dial.

- Equipment
    - 1 large frying pan
    - 2 cutting boards
    - 2 knives
    - 3 small bowls
- Ingredients
    - 1 pound of a beef cut
    - 3 celery stalks
    - 3 medium carrots
    - 2 cups of broccoli, snow/snap peas, or green beans, your choice
    - 1/3 cup soy sauce
    - 2 tablespoons olive oil
    - 1 medium onion
    - 1/2 teaspoon garlic
    - 1 teaspoon basil
    - 1/4 teaspoon black pepper
    - 1/4 teaspoon salt
- Preparation
    - Put pan on burner at medium heat
    - Slice beef into 2" x 1" slices
    - Add olive oil
    - Add spices
    - Add soy sauce
    - Add beef slices
    - Slice carrots, place in bowl 1
    - Turn beef slices
    - Slice celery, place in bowl2
    - Turn beef slices
    - Slice onion, place in bowl 2
    - Turn beef slices
    - Place broccoli (or whatever) in bowl 3
    - Turn beef slices

- Reduce heat to simmer
- Depending on quality of beef cut, cover and simmer for 5-20 minutes
- Return heat to medium high
- Add bowl 1
- Cook for 3 - 5 minutes, stirring or tossing pan occasionally
- Add bowl 2
- Cook for 3 - 5 minutes, stirring or tossing pan occasionally
- Add bowl 3
- Reduce heat to medium
- Cover
- Cook for 3 - 5 minutes, stirring or tossing pan occasionally
- Serve

Seasoned Steak and Mostly Mashed Potatoes

So, steak, we love it, it's delicious. It's also expensive. If you are looking to save money, you can use a less expensive cut of meat you will just need to cook it longer. Since you have to cook it longer, you won't be able to serve it rare. So choose your cut carefully and if you go for a roast-type cut of meat, slice it around 1" thick.

Serve with a vegetable or salad.

- Equipment
    - 2 cutting boards
    - 2 knives
    - 1 large pot
    - 1 large frying pan
    - 1 large spoon
    - Measuring spoons
    - Measuring cups
- Ingredients
    - 2 – 4 steaks or 1 pound of beef cut into 4 portions
    - 2 medium onions
    - 6 small potatoes
    - 1/2 stick of butter
    - 3 tablespoons olive oil
    - 2 teaspoons basil
    - 1 teaspoon garlic
    - 1 teaspoon oregano
    - 1/4 teaspoon black pepper
    - 1/4 teaspoon salt
    - 1/2 cup soy sauce
- Preparation
    - Fill pot 3/4 with water
    - Put pot on burner at high heat
    - Wash potatoes
    - Trim any bad spots off potatoes
    - Leave skin on
    - Dice potatoes
    - Place in pot
    - When water boils, reduce heat to medium, put lid on
    - Cook for 30 minutes, monitor and reduce heat as required to prevent water boiling over
    - Put pan on burner at low heat
    - Add olive oil

- o Add soy sauce
- o Add spices
- o If using less expensive cuts of steak
    - Place cuts into pan
    - Cover
    - Cook for 20 minutes, turning occasionally
    - Remove lid
- o Turn pan to medium high
- o Slice onions
- o Cook steaks to taste
- o Remove steaks
- o Add onions to pan
- o Turn off heat under pot, drain potatoes, leave in pot,
- o Add 1/2 stick of butter to potatoes
- o Toss or stir onions
- o Use large spoon to stir butter and potatoes
- o Remove onions while still crisp
- o Garnish steak
- o Add potatoes to plate
- o Serve

Sliced Pork Medley

This is an approximately 30 minute dish but it's important to remember that it all depends on a continuous flow of effort. While one item is cooking, another item is being prepped and if the prep takes too long, things will be overcooked and bland. So, the first few times you may want to prep all ingredients before you start. After you get the hang of it, impress her with your time and workspace management.

This is a complete meal but you can serve it with hearty bread if desired.

- Equipment
    - 2 cutting boards
    - 2 knives
    - 1 large frying pan
    - Apple corer
    - Melon baller
    - 4 small bowls
    - Measuring spoons
    - Measuring cups
- Ingredients
    - 1 pound of pork
    - 2 medium apples
    - 1 medium pear
    - 2 medium carrots
    - 2 celery stalks
    - 1 medium onion
    - 3 tablespoons olive oil
    - 1/2 cup soy sauce
    - 1 teaspoon garlic
    - 1/2 teaspoon ginger
    - 1/2 teaspoon cinnamon
    - 1/4 teaspoon salt
    - 1/4 teaspoon pepper
    - 1/4 teaspoon sage
    - 1 teaspoon basil
    - 1/2 teaspoon oregano
- Preparation
    - Put pan on burner at medium high heat
    - Add olive oil
    - Put all spices in bowl 1

- Slice pork into 2" x 1" strips
- Add pork
- Add spices
- Slice carrots, put in bowl 2
- Turn pork
- Slice celery, put in bowl 3
- Turn pork
- Slice onion, put in bowl 3
- Turn pork
- Core and slice apples, put in bowl 4
- Confirm pork is nearly done
- Add soy sauce
- Add contents of bowl 2
- Trim pear, slice in half, using the melon baller scoop out seeds, remove stem trail, slice each half lengthwise into 6-8 pieces, place in bowl 3
- Add contents of bowl 3
- Cook 3 minutes, stir or toss pan at least once
- Add contents of bowl 4
- Cook 5 minutes, stir or toss pan at least once
- Remove from heat
- Serve

Home Made Pasta Sauce

This takes a while. You can cook it in an hour but I prefer at least three or four and if you can manage to cook it all day, that's even better. So choose a day you can let it simmer for a while, it's worth the effort. If you like, you can make this a meatless sauce.

As previously mentioned, I use bagged salad because it saves time, I can get a better salad that I like, and I don't waste food.

- Equipment
    - 1 large saucepan
    - 1 frying pan
    - 1 large pot
    - 2 cutting boards
    - 2 knives
- General Ingredients
    - 4 servings of your favourite pasta
- Salad ingredients
    - Bagged salad
    - Salad dressing
    - Grated parmesan cheese
    - Croutons
- Sauce Ingredients
    - 1 29 ounce can tomato puree, unseasoned
    - 1 29 ounce can diced tomatoes, unseasoned
    - 1 medium onion
    - 2 teaspoons basil
    - 1 teaspoon oregano
    - 2 teaspoons garlic
    - 1/2 teaspoon salt
    - 1/4 teaspoon pepper
    - 1/2 teaspoon ginger
- Meat ingredients
    - 1 pound ground beef or pork sausage
    - 1/4 tablespoon salt
    - 1/2 tablespoon pepper
    - 1/2 teaspoon basil
    - 2 tablespoons olive oil
- Preparation
    - Put saucepan on burner at medium high heat
    - Open and empty tomato puree into pan
    - Open and empty diced tomatoes into pan

- o Dice and add onion to pan
- o Add spices to pan
- o Stir occasionally until mixture begins to boil
- o Reduce heat to low, cover
- o Put frying pan on burner at medium heat
- o Add olive oil
- o If using pork sausage, cut into 1" slices
- o Add meat to pan
- o Add spices to pan
- o Brown meat
- o Add meat to sauce
- o Stir sauce occasionally
- o 20 minutes before you are ready to eat
  - Bring water in pot to boil
  - Add pasta
  - Stir pasta occasionally until cooked to taste
- o Open salad
- o Make her salad if you know how she likes it
  - Ask her how she likes her salad if you do not know how she likes it then make her salad
- o Drain pasta
- o Serve

Pan Seared Chicken and Fresh Greens

This is another very quick recipe and by quick I mean around 30 minutes from start to serve. With this in mind, use your time wisely. During cooking time, fill a sink with hot water and soap, stage your dishes, prep place settings, open a bottle of wine, and generally work on your presentation skills. This is a dish that goes excellently with fresh flowers as a "just because" moment.

- Equipment
    - 1 large frying pan
    - 1 cutting board
    - 1 knife
    - 1 small bowl
    - 1 plate
    - Measuring spoons
- Ingredients
    - 2 chicken breasts or 4 chicken thighs (boneless and skinless)
    - 2 tablespoons olive oil
    - 1/4 teaspoon salt
    - 1/4 teaspoon pepper
    - 1/2 teaspoon basil
    - 1/4 teaspoon garlic
    - 1/4 teaspoon onion powder
    - 1 bag of Romaine or other salad
    - Dressing of choice (a balsamic is a safe choice, after that, a Caesar; if you do not know her preference, ask)
    - Croutons, if desired
- Preparation
    - Put pan on burner at medium high heat
    - Add olive oil
    - Add spices to bowl
    - Rinse chicken in cold water and pat dry with paper towels
    - Add spices to pan
    - Add chicken to pan
    - Cook 1 minute
    - While cooking, place used items in dish water
    - Turn chicken over
    - Cook 1 minute
    - Reduce heat to medium

- Turn chicken over
- Cook 2 minutes
- Turn chicken over
- Cook 2 minutes
- While cooking, wash any dirty items and put in dish strainer
- Turn chicken over
- Cook 3 minutes
- While cooking prep salad onto dinner plates
- Turn chicken over
- Cook 3 minutes
- Remove largest piece of chicken from pan, confirm chicken is done by slicing into thickest area, there should be no pink
  - If done, turn off heat, remove all chicken to cutting board
  - If not done, cook an additional 2 - 3 minutes per side
- When chicken is done, slice into 1/2" wide slices
- Place chicken on top of salad greens
- Place salad dressing(s) on table
- Serve

Hobbies

OK guys, it's time to talk about our hobbies.

We're men, we have all sorts of things we like to do, sometimes alone, sometimes with other people, and it is not unusual for these things to have childish aspects and I am here to tell you there is nothing at all wrong with this.

But our hobbies can sometimes be a source of conflict with the women we love. This issue is something we covered right at the beginning of this book, paraphrased to apply to her.

"If you have to change to be the person she wants, she is not the person you want"

If you follow the advice in this book, paying attention to her and noticing her and pampering her and learning to be a real man who can take care of a house and she demands you give up your hobbies I have only one thing to say:

Run.

And this is not a joke in any manner or form. We work, we treat her well, we run a great house, we are the prize at the bottom of the box and she wants us to give up those things that help define who we are and set us apart from the men whose only tactic is to follow her around like a puppy hoping that if they whine enough and are cute enough they might get a pat on the head?

Hell no.

But what if your woman, this great person whom you love and respect and want to be around feels threatened by your hobbies?

Tough.

I know that right now there is at least one person posing the question "but what if my hobby is sleeping with other women?"

Got it, you think you are clever because your mommy always told you so. She was just being polite. We're talking about real hobbies here. We're not talking about stupid, we're talking about sports and collecting and performing and all the other things we men like to do that convince women that we are still children.

Hell we ARE still children. It's part of our charm. It's what keeps us young and makes us want to be better people. Our hobbies are not the only thing that defines us but they certainly make us more interesting and without our hobbies we would never have taken up the ideas in this book.

So gentlemen, your hobbies are important and no one gets to tell you to drop them. Conversely, she has hobbies and you'd damn well better not give her crap about them.

What happens if she doesn't have hobbies? There are two possible reasons she does not have hobbies:

1) She's lying

2) She's boring

Think about it guys, if she has no hobbies then you are her life and we've all had that relationship where every second had to be planned and you begin to wonder why they hell you wanted to be around her in the first place. There is just no amount of pretty to cover that amount of needy.

So support her hobbies even if they are inconvenient and even if it means sometimes she doesn't have time for you because this is not about a weekend, this is about your life. You want someone with whom you can have a conversation 10 years from now.

And so does she.

So your hobbies can't be ignored even if they cause a conflict. You are adults, work it out. Compromise is not a problem as long as there's a balance. If you are always the one compromising it's not compromise, it capitulation.

And all that spells is resentment and the end of a relationship.

Manners

Alright gentlemen, it's time you learned a few things:

- You are not 12, take your hat off at the table
- You are not 12, know the proper use of a knife and fork
- You are not 12, belching at the table is not funny
- You are not 12, licking your plate is not acceptable
- You are not 12, use your napkin
- You are not 12, stop huddling over your food
- You are not 12, don't talk with your mouth full
- You are not 12, whining over the last portion is not tolerated
- You are not 12, "Duuuuude!" is not a proper social greeting
- You are not 12, you can sit still for a movie you do not like
- You are not 12, learn how to shake a hand
- You are not 12, buy a suit
- You are not 12, learn to tie a tie
- You are not 12, dress shoes are required at times
- You are not 12, put the damn toilet seat down
- You are not 12, personal hygiene is not optional
- You are not 12, aim when you use the bathroom
- You are not 12, clean-up if your aim is off
- You are not 12, passing gas is not a sport
- You are not 12, learn to make the bed
- You are not 12, remember to open her door
- You are not 12, remember to hold her chair
- You are not 12, remember to introduce her
- You are not 12, you can say "please" and "thank you"
- You are not 12, don't act like you are

We all have our idiosyncrasies and I am not asking you to stop having a personality, just to not feel like it is your duty to express your manhood by acting as if you are 12 and mad at your mommy.

I've met guys who, in their 30's, brag about their childish manners and I look at the women they are with and think two things:

1) Why does she put up with this?

2) She must be a huge loser to put up with this

If you have such severe oedipal issues that you want your lover to be your mommy, there's nothing I can or want to do for you. If you are looking for someone with whom you can be in a relationship, it's time to learn how to be an adult so that she can introduce you to her friends and co-workers and family without having to say "but he's a really great guy" every time you show them how well you can burp the alphabet.

Because the bad news is that the number of times she will say this is limited and when she reaches that limit, well, she'll be gone and you'll be thinking "but I thought she said I was a great guy!"

She wasn't lying, she was hoping you would learn to be an adult and you didn't so she left.

Does this mean you are an idiot?

Yes, yes it does.

So man up where you need to so you can function as an adult rather than a whiney 12 year old boy who just wants to play X-Box with his "buds" and you don't understand why she wants you to put on a suit to meet her co-workers and why can't you just wear your good jeans and your favourite t-shirt with the dragon on it because it's cool and you are a cool guy and besides she said she liked it.

Even though your mommy puts up with this crap, no woman worth being with will.

It's time to man up and learn to function as an adult where required so you can be a child where it's practical.

It's time to be a man.

Chivalry

Chivalry is a concept and a lifestyle. Chivalry is not sexist because we do not do these things with the belief a woman is incapable of doing them for herself. We do these things because we are gentlemen and we desire to act in a fashion which both highlights this fact and delineates us from the 12 year old boys too busy trying to act like men to be men.

Chivalry must be leavened with practicality. If acting in a chivalrous manner unduly impedes traffic and progress or causes issues, apologise and move on. That we knew what to do and were unable to complete it due to circumstances will in itself set us apart.

Chivalry is more than opening a door and helping her with her coat and going out in the rain to get her umbrella. Chivalry is part of the attitude adjustment. We are deciding to partake of certain actions and attitudes as part of our continued quest for her good opinion and part of our everyday foreplay that inspires her to look at us with both affection and desire.

See, it all comes back to separating her from her clothes; but with style.

With chivalry, you are not concerned with an immediate payback; rather you are concerned with establishing an air about you that, again, gets other people selling you to her. As such, your chivalrous actions will not be limited to just her. This will help you in making the actions part of your lifestyle until they become second nature.

Let's take a moment to list some basics of chivalry in no particular order:

- Opening doors
- Holding chairs
- Retrieving umbrellas and other personal affects (including purse)
- Introducing her
- Getting her a beverage, plate, etc.
- Watching your language in public

- Helping her up and/or down
- Offering her your coat
- Offering her your seat
- Offering her your arm
- Being on time
- Calling her if you are late
- Carrying a handkerchief to offer to her (buy extra, they are inexpensive, she'll remember it each time she sees or uses it)
- Treating her like a lady
- Saying please and thank you to everyone
- Treating all women in a similar manner, remembering she is your first priority

Of course, this is not everything but it should give you an idea of how you want to act in order to be a better man. After all guys, there are billions of men in the world, hundreds to thousands to millions around you and the vast majority of them are acting like 12 year old boys as they try to impress each other in hopes that some vapid girl will like them.

You win this game by not playing. Be the exception so you can attract and keep the exceptional women.

A word of caution, however; you are acting in a chivalrous manner because it is how you want to act. She is not due this treatment, you are due this attitude. Your first motivation is your own attitude and thus you do this without expectation of reciprocal treatment. That's the long way of saying, "don't keep score." Twelve times opening a door does not equate to anything. As soon as you assign a value above "I do this because it makes me feel good" then you are wasting everyone's time.

And lastly, if you are doing these things and they are not enough, run. There's a wide gulf between appreciation and expectation and a wider one between appreciation and demands. If she demands more you will have to decide how miserable you want to be to have her in your company.

It's not about being right, it's about being happy.

Boys Night Out

Guys, I'm here to tell you that Boys Night Out is not only acceptable, but required and if the woman you are with complains about it, run. If she demands you ask permission, run. If she treats it as a burden, figure this out now because it will be brought up in a fight later.

Of course, this assumes Boys Night Out is a once a week or so thing, not 3+ nights a week and that you refrain from engaging in certain classes of stupid that you know would make you angry if she did them.

But a night out with the guys will aid you in several ways. You'll get to relax with your friends, always a good thing. You'll get ogle other women without consequence, always a good thing. But most of all you'll get to hear the stories from the other guys about how crappy their relationships are and you'll be reminded how lucky you are and why you want to do the things in this book in the first place because you could be with one of the soul-sucking harpies that your friends have ended up with because that is the only woman who will tolerate grown men who behave as if they are spoiled children.

It's funny because it's true. It's pathetic because it is true. It's true because, well, it's true.

So if you don't have a Boys Night Out, plan one. Do something, get out of the house, give her some space, let her know that you care deeply for her but still have those qualities and interests that first attracted her to you.

Be a man, not a boy.

And if the question "What did you guys do?" arises, the only answer you have to give is "I did nothing stupid." If you want to say more, it is your choice but you do not have to explain every action you take and this is never about asking permission; you just have to not act in a stupid manner. If she can't trust you to not act stupidly and feels the need to check up on you, what are you doing with her in the first place?

Girls Night Out

This is a goose and gander thing. You want her to have a Girls Night Out and if it does not coincide with Boys Night Out, that's even better because that means two evenings you are away from each other. This is a good thing.

We are guys and at times we will want to do things in which she has zero interest and, quite honestly, the same applies to her. This is not bad, this is making certain each of you maintain aspects of your lives and remain the people who first attracted each other. You'll be doing plenty together so a couple of nights a week apart will not kill either of you.

But you want her to go out with her friends for another reason. Her friends will all be talking about the man-child in their life and how annoying he is and how he never does anything around the house and only talks to her when he wants sex and thinks foreplay is getting undressed and she'll tell them about you and you will be a hero.

All for doing the things you should be doing all along.

And so when you have a bad day or week or month and you and the woman in your life are under some stress, her girlfriends will be reminding her what a wonderful man you are or scheming to steal you away from her and either one serves to make her reconsider brash actions.

This is a good thing. Brash actions can cause serious problems and often involve tear-soaked apologies that leave you both wondering what went wrong even when it is painfully obvious because of the action in question.

So, Girls Night Out; support it and don't ask questions about it. If you can't trust that she did nothing stupid, what are you doing with her in the first place?

Boundaries

Guys, we need to talk about boundaries. Boundaries are acceptable behavior you and the woman in your life have agreed upon. The critical point is "agreed upon." These are not things she has dictated to you or you have dictated to her. Adults have conversations and adults are not threatened by the unimportant.

Using myself as an example, I am an incurable flirt and I remain in absolute awe of the female parts. So any woman who is in my life has to understand that I will notice that other women are beautiful and I will admire the form of other women and I will flirt incessantly. I make this clear up front but I also make certain of one thing. I never give a better compliment to another woman than I do to the woman in my life. Remember this, it is important. You are allowed to notice that other women are stunning and desirable and you do not have to find an artificial flaw with them, you just have to remember that we are all insecure and not be an idiot about it.

After all, you are not a 12 year old boy who is looking for his first glimpse of a female breast; you are a man, act like it. When you look at other women, look, don't gawk. When you compliment other women, compliment them to the woman with you and then kiss her hand or give her a hug. If you've been following the advice in this book, you can notice other women because you are noticing her more.

And what if she has a problem that you notice other women? Run.

Seriously, we've covered this. Jealousy is not cute, it's insecurity and will spiral out of control until you are answering accusations and lying to her because you don't want to have THAT conversation again and some of you will even start violating the boundaries because you are so tired of it all but do not have the spine to end the relationship and instead find some bizarre justification for your behavior in your 12 year old brain.

So you will need to establish early that your hormones do not shut down and that you can find other women attractive without having to pursue them and, this is critical, you can't be jealous when she finds other men attractive.

The woman in your life is allowed to notice other men. She will notice their look and their posture and their smell and she might even be so taken by some aspect of them that she will mention it to you.

Man up and deal with it. If you can't stand the fact that there are other men in the world while you have her in your life, you are a 12 year old boy and when she leaves you it should be no surprise but will be because you are stuck at 12.

So, that's the everyday boundaries but, of course, there are more.

Society has some general distinctions as to what is and is not acceptable behavior. I'm not too very concerned with that and will tell you that you and she should talk and establish acceptable and clear behavioral boundaries. These are not imposed, these are discussed and negotiated and understood by everyone and, most of all, they are equal.

Perhaps it's just me but I do not desire to run another person's life. Hell, I've got all I can handle with my own, though I'm not willing to cede its control to anyone. This means I am looking for an adult relationship with someone who has a life, has a viewpoint, has hobbies, has direction, and has a desire to run their own damn life.

You don't have to agree on everything, but you have to have a boundary framework in place so you both can concentrate on the relationship rather than the reasons you are justifiably angry. Because gentlemen, being justifiably angry is still being angry and is consuming time you could be doing things that convinces her to shed her clothes.

So talk about boundaries and for God's sake, don't violate them. When you do all you are saying is that you want the relationship to be over. If you are done with the relationship, be a man, end the relationship. She deserves better and if you do, what are you doing sticking around?

Wasting the time of all involved, that's what.

Gifts and Holidays

Alright gentlemen, it's time to get some things straight. It is not difficult to buy the woman in your life a gift and you do not have to spend a fortune to make her happy unless you are an idiot and have not recorded the following information:

- Her allergies
- Her shoe size
- Her ring size
- Her measurements
- Her favourite color, gemstone, precious metal, flower, animal, fabric, hot beverage, cold beverage, and alcoholic beverage
- Her least favourite color, gemstone, precious metal, flower, animal, fabric, hot beverage, cold beverage, and alcoholic beverage

Wow, that's a lot and it's not even everything. How can you possibly be expected to know this or even remember it?

First you ask; then you write it down. You ask her, her friends, her parents, and her siblings. If you want to be sneaky, check the labels of her clothing. But you always write it down. What's more, you write it into the Notes section of the contact information for her on your phone. Now you have it wherever you are.

Once you have this information, gifts become easier because, surprise, you know what she likes. If she likes cats, you can get cat-themed items including charms and perfume bottles. If she loves cashmere, a cashmere scarf is a great gift, as long as it is the right color but luckily you wrote that down.

Since you won't be standing around with the other idiots thinking "But what does she like?" you won't overspend on something she'll return. Now, she may still return it, she is a woman, after all, but at least you'll have picked the right color and size.

And this, gentlemen, is the key to the whole gift giving process. By knowing what she likes and does not like, you no longer have to buy her the same damn thing as everyone else or, worse, the current over-priced crap piece of jewelry that has been deemed the next "must have" item to prove you love her. Because the more the woman in your life sees another woman with the same piece of jewelry you bought her, the more annoyed she becomes. What's worse, she may not even know why she is annoyed but you will see that overpriced trendy panic purchase relegated to her jewelry box and a vague discontent settle over the item and when you bring it up in a discussion you will be surprised at the vitriolic reaction.

Admit it, you've been there. You've been there because you did not follow the first rule, "Notice her."

Gifts should build on the connection between you both. They should express the fact that you notice her and know what she likes. This is the reason small gifts frequently given are better than make-up gifts or, worse yet, guilt gifts panic bought because you forgot one of the four major holidays.

What? You didn't realise that there were four major holidays? Let's cover those in order of importance.

Anniversary

It's time for more bad news. You have an anniversary even if you do not think you have an anniversary. If you are not married, you have a first date or first kiss or first something anniversary and forgetting it is a quick way to find yourself at the wrong end of her anger and disappointment.

Now, women go overboard with anniversaries and I am not telling you to support the obsession, just be aware of the situation so that you can respond. The woman in your life may remind you of a one month and three month and six month anniversary. Know that she might do this but ignore the dates. It's unreasonable to celebrate a relationship that is not a relationship and even if you have honestly decided you plan to spend a significant portion of your life with her, supporting these faux anniversaries is just sending a mixed message that will come back to bite you. Yearly anniversaries are different.

You need to know the date of your yearly anniversary but only the anniversary of your first date or your marriage or something in line with this. Yes you can write down the date of every other first but, trust me; you are setting yourself up for failure. What you want to do is establish that you know a specific date and why it is important and ignore any other faux anniversary dates or circumstances.

For your anniversary you will schedule a yearly recurring appointment on your calendar and include in the appointment information the original date and circumstances of the anniversary including the year it began. This way when there is a numerically significant anniversary, you will be prepared. And what is numerically significant? The one year, five year, 10 year, 20, 30, etc. It's not that difficult; it just takes a plan. So plan.

You are not allowed to ask her what she wants for an anniversary present because if you do you are shouting, "THIS IS NOT IMPORTANT, I'M JUST DOING IT TO APPEASE YOU." And even if that is the case, it's stupid to tell her. If the date is not important to you, focus on the fact that she is important to you and this date is important to her so treat it with respect.

Jewelry is always a good idea for anniversaries as it is personal and denotes permanence to the relationship. Rings are not my first choice but you are welcome to try them. Necklaces or earrings are good and a bracelet, especially a charm bracelet is a great idea. With a charm bracelet you are securing ideas for future gifts and chronicling your relationship with her.

If you feel you must get her lingerie, make certain you get her something else since we all know we buy her lingerie for its effect on us. Hell, even if she loves lingerie, congratulations if that is the case, you will want to buy her a gift that she can show off outside intimate occasions.

Her Birthday

Oh the dangers of her birthday. Whenever you feel inspired to get her a gag gift highlighting her age, stop, slam your testicles in a door, and when you recover, don't be such an idiot next time. Women are sensitive about their age. Understand this and do not be a moron.

Celebrate her birthday, on time or early, but never late. This means you will be scheduling another recurring event in your calendar. And while you are allowed to ask her what she would like for her birthday, it's really better if you have enough information from noticing and appreciating her to know what will make a good gift.

Lingerie is not a good gift on her birthday since, as we have already discussed, it is something you most likely wanted her to have so you could see her in it, however briefly. Avoid any self-help product as well; books, exercise equipment, etc. A spa treatment or gift certificate for a manicure or pedicure is a great idea. And, as always, there is jewelry, just don't use it as a crutch instead of thinking of things she will appreciate more.

When you decide on a card, start with a blank card and write her something, anything, telling her why she is special, why you love her, why she is beautiful and alluring and desirable. Use the birthday card to remind her that you find her more attractive than ever.

Why? It's because women are sensitive about their age and you want to reassure her that you see the absolute best in her and look forward to as many more birthdays as are possible. Her birthday is a great time to let her know, through your attention, that you plan to be there for her, forever.

Valentine's Day

I don't have anything good to say about Valentine's Day aside from it is the birthday of one of my sons. I despise the concept, the circumstances, the expectations, and the execution of Valentine's Day. There is not a single thing about Valentine's Day as a holiday that I like or support.

But even I never forget Valentine's Day.

But we catch a break here. Since you are engaging in your relationship on a daily basis, the pressure around Valentine's Day is significantly reduced. Yes you will get her a card but make it a blank card and write her a note or a poem. Get her flowers too, but not roses unless that is her favourite flower and if it is, don't get just roses, get an arrangement of roses and other things that she likes. Gift wise, make it simple, not extravagant. Extravagance on Valentine's Day is a way to say "I don't know what to do; I hope this is right because all the other boys are doing it." Show thought, not just money.

You are never allowed to ask her what she wants for Valentine's Day. Lingerie is acceptable on Valentine's Day but should always be accompanied with another gift. Except for charms, I normally avoid jewelry on Valentine's Day since it's the panic gift men buy when they can think of nothing else.

An unexpected outing to something she loves is better than squeezing into an overcrowded restaurant with everyone else. Take her to dinner another day just because, make Valentine's about your relationship rather than about the standard "Flowers, Chocolate, Dinner, Jewelry, Sex" checklist.

These are the types of things that will set you apart, that will show her that you notice her and appreciate her and want to pamper her. This is what separates you from the herd of boys stumbling around hoping someone will notice them and will state plainly you are a real man.

Christmas or Other Winter Holiday

Firstly, I celebrate Christmas. If you do not, apply this advice to the holiday you celebrate around this time of year or skip the section entirely.

This is the easiest of all holidays. You get to ask her what she wants, there's never any question as to when it is, and expectations are fairly low since it is a shared and not a personal celebration. It's not a holiday that is about your relationship, it's a cultural celebration and as such the rules are looser and it's harder to fail.

Luckily, you have your contact information handy with its list of her information so that when you go shopping, you are prepared, unlike those other guys stumbling from Victoria's Secret to the jewelry store hoping they will hit the right combination of expense and guilt to inspire physical contact.

And while this is an acceptable time for practical gifts, tread lightly. If she asked for exercise equipment or gym membership, you are allowed to get it for her. If she did not, avoid making that mistake.

Clothing is usually a good choice and since you have her measurements and color preferences, now is the time to put those to full use and select gifts that will cause her friends to compliment her so she can tell them it was a gift from you so they can tell her what a wonderful and thoughtful man you are and they wish their man was as smart because maybe then they would not have gotten a colander; for the third time in three years.

Gifts in General

There are some things that should never be given as a gift; appliances, cleaning supplies, self-help products she did not request, live animals, and anything you want more than she does.

If your household needs an appliance, it's for both of you, no matter how much it costs it is not a gift and the same thing applies to that special mop or broom or whatever you saw on TV no matter what host said what about it. Newsflash; they are getting paid to look happy; it does not make it a gift. Ever.

If she did not ask for a self-help book or piece of equipment, giving it to her screams, "I do not like you the way you are." This is not the purpose of a present. If there is an issue you should be talking about it and while we will cover that more in depth shortly, the important thing to remember is that if you are trying to make her feel guilty with a gift, well, then, you are an idiot.

As far as live animals, it does not matter if she really wanted a puppy three years ago, it's best to broach the subject BEFORE you find out she changed her mind and does not want to invest the time and energy right now. Otherwise, each time there is a mess or an issue or a bill, it will remind her that you do not pay attention to her or know what she likes or wants. Don't be that guy.

And lastly, before you decide you'll kill two birds with one stone by getting her a new TV or computer or free weight set or whatever, realise that if you do this you are announcing that you are 12 years old and she will use this as a story to her family and friends about how you don't understand her and remind her of the little boy who got his mother a baseball glove "for them both to use." It will be cute and adoring right up to the point it becomes the last straw and is thrown at you as one more example of how you are an idiot.

Fashion

I will be the very first to admit I neither understand nor like fashion, fad, or the vast majority of popular culture. So how can I give you advice on fashion?

Easy, I pay attention and I have a plan.

If you have a fashion sense, or if you are comfortable in a lifestyle that precludes these types of fashions, ignore this section or read it and chuckle over my simplistic advice. If, like me, fashion is a word you use mostly in derision, pay attention, we'll make this nearly painless.

There are three main types of fashion about which you have to worry:

1) Casual

2) Business Casual

3) Formal

Let's cover them in order:

Work Clothes

Wait, that's not on the list. I know; it's because work clothes follow no fashion rules. Most of my work clothes are casual clothes that have seen better days and I no longer worry about rips or tears or stains. I just make certain my work clothes allow me to go to the hardware store without embarrassment. After that, all bets are off.

Casual

Casual wear is the thing you wear as a default. Jeans, t-shirts, sneakers, fleece, hoodies, etc. The rule here is that it should be clean (see "Laundry" in the previous chapters) and that it should be in good repair.

"Does this mean I can't wear my ripped jeans?"

Yes, that's exactly what it means. If you are over 25, act like it. If you are over 25 and are wearing ripped jeans because you think they make you look cool, I have some bad news. They do not make you look cool, they make you look like you want people to think you are cool and so are trying the same thing that worked for you 5, 10, 20, or more years ago.

If it sounds pathetic it's because it is pathetic.

For jeans, find a brand that's versatile enough to become work jeans when they show their age but also serve as your default pants of choice and look decent enough to wear out on a less formal date, be acceptable for casual days at work, etc., and have at least three pair.

For shirts you have a wide choice; t-shirts, casual button-down, fleece, sweatshirts, hoodies, etc. The same rules apply here. Nothing ripped, nothing torn, and if it's the style to be ripped or torn and you are over 25, you look stupid. Insert previous caveat about a lifestyle fashion here. I don't like to accidently offend people, where's the fun in that?

Oh, and that t-shirt with the pornographic saying? It's not funny, it's not sexy, it's not clever, and it does not show you are a rebel. It shows you are 12 and while it's fine for a 12 year old, it's not fine for us. Step up; get clothes she won't be ashamed of you wearing when she introduces you to her boss or parents.

As far as shoes go, just make certain they are in good repair. Duct tape on our shoes when we are in college is innovative and clever. When you are over 25 it's sad and pathetic. Just because your feet have stopped growing and you spent $200 on a pair of sneakers you love, putting tape on them only says you are an idiot who can't manage his money. Next time spend $50 and buy a spare set and have $100 left over use in a wiser manner.

A lot of your casual wear clothes will devolve into your work clothes and that's a great plan. It saves you money and it saves you time.

As far as coats, your options are wide open. Windbreakers, dusters, parkas, whatever makes you happy. Again, keep it in good repair because nothing screams "Look, I am 12!" like not being able to part with a broken down coat. As for patches and stickers and nearly any other sort of decoration, get rid of them. I know you love Star Wars or Star Trek but you are not a Jedi and you never attended Star Fleet Academy. Let it go.

Except for the jeans and coat, you should plan on updating your casual clothes at least once every three years. Keep the t-shirts you don't regret, give the rest to charity and update your wardrobe with newer things you do not hate.

This way you are always in the correct decade for what is considered fashionable without ever having to pay attention to fashion.

Business Casual

Many work places have a business casual dress policy. This consists of slacks and polo shirts and button down shirts and sweaters and semi-dress to dress shoes.

Business casual is a tough call and I admit I do not enjoy it; so I cheat.

Sure I have at least four pair of slacks and so should you. These could be chinos or Dockers or what-the-hell-ever they are being called now-a-days but are really just non-jean items that are not part of a suit.

After that, I have a lot of button down shirts that I wear with my casual clothes. They are not dress shirt quality and I follow the same three year policy with replacing them and my slacks.

If you are absolutely in love with blazers, this is when you wear them. You can wear them in lieu of a jacket, you can wear them to dress up a pair of decent looking jeans; you can even wear them with a tie and button down shirt. Business casual can be versatile even though I find it cumbersome.

As for shoes, personally, I wear my dress shoes. It's not only because I am lazy, it's because dress shoes look better and wear better than a lot of the "casual" shoes and this practice allows me to have around five pair of general use shoes in my closet. If you love shoes, buy as many as you want.

As far as coats go for business casual you can get away with using your casual coat as long as you have gotten rid of those patches and stickers and what-not. You can also get away with using whatever coat you have for your formal wear. The choice is yours, have at it.

Formal

Formal wear is probably the easiest of the wardrobe classifications.

You need suits. Not blazers and slacks, suits. You want at least two suits and you want to plan on buying another suit at least once every five years though a new suit every three years is better.

You want a natural fiber suit. Linen and wool are the classic choices for their look and their wear-ability. Linen suits are normally worn when the weather is warmer, wool when it is cooler though you can wear a lightweight wool suit in the summer with no problem. A linen suit in cold weather will most probably look a trifle odd and be very chilly.

You want dress-quality shirts. Long sleeve only. I don't care what you wear for work; you want a long sleeve shirt for your suit; anything else is a waste of effort. These will be 100% cotton and should be professionally cleaned because they look better and wear better and last longer. Classic colors are your best choice here. Solid white and solid blue, vertical stripes if that catches your fancy, and avoid any plaid or paisley or what-the-hell-ever trend. If you like cufflinks, go for it. If you do not, don't worry about it.

As for shoes, they should be leather and leather soled. If you object to the use of animal products, make your own damn choice. Leather shoes take a richer and deeper shine and leather soles give you a firmer and quieter step. Leather rarely marks a floor and when you have your legs crossed and people see the soles of your shoes, leather does not embarrass you with "pithy" sayings.

Ties are a personal preference. Choose carefully and have at least two ties for every suit. Ties should be replaced every three years. Even if the pattern is not dated, the width of fashionable ties will differ each year and they begin to look dated after a few years have passed.

You will need a topcoat or trench coat. Your top coat should be natural fiber and I recommend a cashmere and wool blend for durability, look, and feel. An important thing to remember when you choose your top or trench coat is that you will be wearing a suit with it. A suit has a jacket. The woman in your life may be wearing something formal in nature that highlights all the parts of her you most enjoy. These outfits are often not overly warm.

Plan ahead; spend the extra money on a nice top or trench coat that she will love to wear because it is warm and feels luxurious and smells like you. It's little things like this that remind her in ways she does not even realise that you are special and she is lucky to be in your life.

Basics

You should have several leather belts, yes, leather. You'll need two for business casual/formal and two for casual. The former should be replaced every two years, the latter are replaced when they wear out or you hate them.

Be very aware of the belt buckles you choose. Make certain before you put them on they are telling people what you want them to know about you.

Also, I did not mention underwear or undershirts or socks. These are personal preferences and should follow a single rule; they should be in good repair. Good repair means that if it has holes, it's time for it to become part of your work clothes or a rag. Colors for any of these are a personal choice but it's good to remember a white t-shirt is always a good decision under a button down shirt and that your socks may be visible and black will rarely let you down.

The Rest

No, I said nothing about black tie and white tie and all sorts of things but we need to keep this simple and if you are involved in a lifestyle that supports additional fashion considerations, seek the advice of someone more qualified than I am on this.

Ask her, she'll love it.

Walking

This is more important than you will believe and you do not even notice what you are doing; hell, I didn't for years. We are guys, we go from point A to point B and we clear the way for those who follow in our wake and it's up to them to keep pace.

Yeah, think about that for a second and imagine the look of exasperation on her face as she walks three to five steps behind you. You'll have to imagine because you can't see it as you are ignoring her and causing her to wonder where the fire is and why you need to walk so fast and are you ashamed to be seen with her and do you think she's fat.

Here's a newsflash; women like to hold hands when walking. If you can hold their hand when you are 10 feet in front of them, you are still doing it incorrectly, though impressively. Part of the hand holding experience for her is a joy of being near you and part is a territorial thing, letting everyone know you are with her. By leaving her in your wake you are giving her doubts.

So slow down and walk with her, talk with her, hold her hand.

But what if you do not really like holding hands while walking? No worries, I've got you covered since I'm not much of a hand-holder when walking. Take her hand and put it in the crook of your arm, laying your other hand on top of it. This is more intimate than holding hands and more sophisticated and more comfortable and you get to caress her hand occasionally. That's a win.

When you walk with her you can ask her about her day, her thoughts, her stance on global warming, or whatever else strikes her fancy. But by walking with her in physical contact you satisfy her territorial desires and let her know she is important to you and you do not look like an idiot and she does not have use up one of those "but he's a really great guy" markers.

They are not infinite, after all, so save them for something important and slow down and walk with her.

Dancing

Let me guess, you only slow dance.

Idiot.

If you are not comfortable with the modern concept of dancing, fine, I fairly despise it myself. So take some lessons.

Take Swing Dance lessons, Ballroom, Salsa, whatever you both like that will get you out on the dance floor with her in your arms and enjoying herself.

Here's the thing about dancing. It's erotic, it's great exercise, and it is high intensity foreplay that is not only acceptable in public but for which you will be universally lauded.

And it gives you something to do in the living room or kitchen or store or wherever else you might be when you are bored or interested or whatever. It's like talking about the weather but with a point. It's like watching TV but with a lot of touching. It's like telling her that you enjoy her company so much you love to spontaneously take her hand and see that sparkle in her eyes.

If you are so concerned about what your friends will say about you taking dancing lessons, turn in your man card and relegate yourself to dating insecure and needy women for the rest of your life because you will never keep a real woman interested in you since you are more concerned with boys thinking you are a man than actually being a man. And hey, if that's all you want, patter along and play Nintendo and have your Hot Pocket. She'll find someone who is both interesting and interested in her and you'll wonder what happened since everyone always thought you were cool.

What happened is simple; you are not 12 years old any longer. Spending time in extended public foreplay with that special woman should be more important to you than what your friends might say to you as they are scheming to find a girl who is half the woman your girl is.

Dance, it's good for you, it's good for her, and it's good for the relationship.

Massages

It's time for more bad news guys. We think we are being clever when we offer to massage that special woman in our life. We are not be clever, we are being transparent and fixated and she knows it and, worse, she begins to associate any touch from us with our desire to get her naked.

The tragedy is, of course, she is right.

So we need to understand the difference between a sensual massage and an "I love you and want to make you feel better but expect nothing of you" massage. And no, they are not the same. If you want to use a sensual massage during lovemaking – go for it; just make certain you actually know what she likes. Do this by asking her. It is a radical concept, true, but has been known to both work and save time.

Now, what she will appreciate most is a non-sensual massage because you can do this both in public and without causing her to cringe when she is tired or distracted or not in the mood for sex.

A quick guide to a non-sensual massage is that it involves non-sensual areas that are publicly acceptable to touch. Think of the areas below the elbow, below the knee, the temples, and the neck. Basically, these are places you might touch a female friend without getting her angry or a male friend might touch her without upsetting you; much. Think back to boundaries for this.

The wonderful thing about these non-sensual massages is that they get her to associate your touch with comfort and security and not just sex. We've covered this before guys but when a woman thinks the only reason you touch her is to have sex, she will be much less responsive. And even though we nearly always want to separate her from her clothes, we're men, not 12 year old boys, so we can invest in some touching that does not immediately result in sex. And yes, that means non-sensual massages become yet another form of foreplay.

You are very welcome.

Finances

This will be short.

- Maintain separate bank accounts, always.
- Create a budget.
- If she makes more than you, split household expenses 50/50.
- If you make more than her, prorate her contribution to household expenses to the nearest 5%. How do you prorate? Divide the larger salary into the smaller salary, subtract that number from 1. Add that number to your 50% and that is the percentage of the bill you will be paying.

Here's your formula:

- X = her salary
- Y = your salary
- Z = the bill to be paid
- $(1-(X/Y) +.5) * Z =?$
- $(1 - (30,000/35,000) + .5 * 100) = 65$

So you pay $65 of the bill of $100.

Isn't this sexist? Yes it is and I do not really care, do it.

What if you really want a joint bank account? You are an idiot.

What if she really wants a joint bank account? No.

What if it will really, really make her happy? Are you listening? The answer is "No," no matter the inducement. "Hell no" comes easily to mind here.

What if only one of you works outside the home? Set up a per paycheck sum to be deposited in an account to run the house and pay the bills. It's like having a budget because it's having a budget.

It's a budget thing, learn to understand.

Guilt and Apologies

Guilt is complicated so we are going to make this as simple as possible. Guilt is a useless response to a situation. Remorse is one thing and as a man when you do something wrong you respond by doing three things:

1) Acknowledge your mistake, immediately

2) Apologise sincerely, immediately

3) Make appropriate amends, immediately

And that's it. You don't engage in guilt because you have been a real man and done what you could to address and reconcile the situation. Oh, and a present is not amends, changing your behavior if it is wrong is amends. When gifts are associated with guilt, you are well and truly screwed.

Now of course, you will have to understand that there are certain classes of stupid that preclude this type of approach and, most importantly, this approach usually works only once per type of error. That is the polite way of saying it is not a cure all for you constantly doing the same moronic thing over and over and expecting your winning smile, ready "sorry", and random gifts will mean all is forgiven. If this is your strategy, remember, there are a finite "but he's a great guy" cards and once you consume them, she's gone.

So, what are the major classes of stupid? Remember the discussion on boundaries? Anytime you violate those, it is a major class of stupid; it might be an end-of-relationship class of stupid so it is important to refrain from being an idiot by violating them. If you are still uncertain about the boundaries in your relationship, it's time to have a talk and understand them because, and we have all been there, it is no fun having a conversation through a closed door about something you were supposed to know. You can't even sincerely apologise in this situation as all you can do is say you are sorry over and over and hope she will tell you why.

But that brings up the flip side of the whole guilt and apology situation.

Let's say you are avoiding the major classes of stupid, great. Let's say you are noticing and appreciating and pampering her, perfect. Let's say you have remembered all of the holidays, wonderful. Let's say you previously made a mistake, owned up to it, sincerely apologised, made amends, and moved on, beautiful. Then let's say the woman in your life constantly mentions some incident hoping to make you feel guilty and thus manipulate you.

Not OK, ever.

If something happened and you made amends and she told you it was OK or forgiven and whatever happened never happened again, there is no need for guilt and any attempt at guilt is manipulation. Guys, if your woman believes manipulation is part of a relationship, it is a huge problem.

Adults talk, adults compromise, adults do not scheme to play on the emotions of others in hopes of manipulating them into complying with whatever whim they are currently experiencing. And that is all the use of guilt is; manipulation. No one who cares for you will believe manipulating you is a viable long-term relationship strategy.

She can tell you her concerns, she can tell you what she wants, and she is even allowed to hint. She is not allowed to try to manipulate you through guilt because that is not a relationship; that is a train-wreck.

And gentlemen, neither of you are allowed to use the "if you loved me . . ." ploy. Because the translation of any "if you loved me . . ." conversation is:

"I don't care about you, I just you to do what I want, NOW!"

And if this conversation is a constant of your relationship, your relationship sucks.

The moral is, don't do the stupid things. You'll have enough minor issues throughout your relationship to keep you busy with admitting guilt and making amends and, truthfully, she will as well. The difference is that a boy will engage in stupidity and thoughtlessly hurt others. A man will learn what is acceptable and what is not in a relationship. So, if the relationship is important to you, man up and learn the difference between remorse and guilt.

If the relationship is not important to you, she deserves better than you.

Fighting

You are going to have disagreements and at times these disagreements will spill over into arguments and these will spill over into fights and before you know it you have a great opportunity to royally screw things up.

People handle anger differently and I will not tell you to how to fight, I will tell you how to avoid having the same fight.

If you've split up the housework and you are doing your share, you won't have to fight about chores. If you've drawn up a budget and are adhering to it, you won't have to fight about money. If you've clearly established boundaries and are following them, you won't have to fight about these misunderstandings and transgressions.

But there will be plenty of other opportunities for fighting. It is inevitable in any relationship. There are two main things to remember when you are upset:

1. There are important things and there are unimportant things; choose carefully

2. Words can't be unsaid, actions can't be undone

If you feel tempted to use words to hurt her because you feel hurt and angry, stop. Tell her that you are upset but need to think. Let her know you need 15 minutes to calm down, then take 15 minutes and calm down and construct a reasonable response that does not involve using words or phrases you desperately hope are not an accurate description of this woman.

If she refuses to agree to this it is a warning sign that, no matter what else she is, she may be the wrong brand of crazy for you. If she is yelling and screaming, tell her she is welcome to continue yelling and screaming at you until she feels better but you are taking 15 minutes to calm down because you love her and don't want to lose sight of it.

If this makes her angry, it's another warning sign.

At the root of it though is this; if something is annoying you, bring it up early in a non-accusatory manner. Do not wait for days or weeks or months or years and then erupt over her spilling the salt. Be a man, talk to her. And what do I mean by a non-accusatory manner? Let's demonstrate.

Accusatory:

You don't understand my point.

Non-accusatory:

I'm not explaining my point very well.

The accusation is much more likely to lead to a fight than the non-accusation. You are already upset and the chances are that she is already upset so you need to choose words that do more than just hurt.

Because do you know what's better than make-up sex? Not going a week or more with her not touching you, not kissing you, shying away from you, and generally ignoring you because you've been an idiot.

And what if you find yourself having the exact same fight over and over? Well, you need to admit something is seriously wrong. If you are being reasonable, then she is being unreasonable and vice versa. If you both think you are acting reasonably, it may be time for a third party to get involved.

Luckily, that's covered in the next chapter.

Counselling

"But I did everything right, what's wrong with her?"

Remember the previous chapter on fighting? That's a horrible way to ask the question.

"I feel like I am doing my best and I love her but we still fight and are upset at each other all the time. What can I do?"

You can look into counseling.

Counseling is not an admission of failure or weakness, it's an acknowledgement that your relationship with her is valuable and important and even though it is off-track right now you believe it is worth the work to make it right.

OK, so we admit a counselor might be a good idea, what next?

Make sure it is the right counselor.

You put a lot of thought into your mechanic, your plumber, electrician, contractor, etc. This is even more important than finding the right mechanic. This is about finding that person who can work with both of you to help identify issues and solutions.

If the counselor is taking sides, that is a problem. Now, this assumes you are doing the things we have outlined in this guide. You are doing 50ish percent of the housework, you are cleaning up after yourself, you are cooking, you are shedding bad manners, you are supporting her hobbies, and you are letting her know you care for her as more than a destination for physical satiation. It also assumes you are not acting stupidly. If you are continuously drinking to excess or not working or violating the boundaries of your relationship, fix that first because otherwise you are wasting time and money.

When I talk about taking sides, I mean that the counselor will determine one person is always the problem and this may be a sign that the counselor is a moron. Hey, it happens. No profession is immune to its share of morons and the whole psychology and/or psychiatric field is no exception. The goal is to find someone who will listen, who will mediate, and who will offer concrete suggestions and strategies to help the relationship heal and grow.

This will mean both of you have to be open and honest and willing to entertain that change might be required. If you are just attending counseling because she "made" you then you are, yes, an idiot. The goal here is not to "get through" these issues, the goal is to lay a foundation so you can both solve the issues and if you cannot be honest then you are just your wasting time and money. And trust me; if you are looking to waste money, there are much better things on which to do so.

During counseling sessions and exercises you may learn or reveal some hurtful things. Be prepared to deal with them as calmly as possible. During the sessions you may also learn something that happened before you knew her, either in childhood or early adulthood or whatever is still plaguing her and you are the lucky recipient of the trauma.

If she is willing to work on resolving those issues, great. Be there for her. If she or the counselor insists you must perform some sort of mental and emotional gymnastics in order to assuage this sensitive spot, no.

No only no, but hell no.

Not only hell no but, perhaps, goodbye.

Again, this is not a joke in any way, shape or form. It's not about loving her enough, it's about taking responsibility and we cannot take responsibility for the harm caused by or the flaws of others. It's too much and it is unfair to ask of anyone.

Here's the brutal truth. Everyone has had a rough life and nothing in her past gives her the right to treat you poorly. If she has intimacy issues due to some horrific thing that happened in her life, you have to decide how miserable you are willing to be for how long so that you can hope that one day she wants to touch your penis.

We all have issues. Some are minor, some are major, but none of them are the responsibility of other people to fix or support. When people know they have an issue and refuse to address it they are stating that the comfort they get from their actions is worth any inconvenience or harm those actions cause to themselves or others.

Which brings us back to the "how miserable for how long" question. Sometimes, despite what you want, need, hope, and yearn for, sometimes a relationship can't be fixed. Sometimes it can't even be defined. Sometimes it just needs to end.

This is one reason it is important to identify the right brand of crazy from the start so that even if you have to go to counseling you are both on the same page as to the end result. Hell, you call in a professional to help you with other areas of your life, so don't be a 12 year old boy about this, if the relationship is important find someone who can help and make an effort.

And guys, if you are the one with the unresolved issues and you are using them as an excuse to behave in a manner that is driving her away and you are the one expecting her to stick around to be treated like crap, well, you are an idiot and you don't deserve her and it's just a matter of time before the last "but he's a great guy" marker is consumed and she is gone.

You are an adult; it's time to get past the issues in childhood. It's time to stop using them as an excuse to be stupid. It's time to make changes or settle for being miserable and lonely or worse, miserable and with the wrong brand of crazy, one failed relationship at a time.

Yeah, you know these people, don't be them.

The Art of the Compliment

Hey, is this where the title of the book developed? Yes, yes it is. So let's get to it, shall we?

The secret of a good compliment is that it should be personal. It should define a connection between you and the person receiving the compliment. They should realise that what you are telling them is heartfelt and sincere.

"You're very pretty" is something you say to your dog and something she hears from people every day so you need to stand out and it is easier than you think.

Everything that has come before this chapter is part of the foundation to a good compliment, especially one of the first things we discussed:

Notice her.

Your goal should be to give her a compliment that lets her know you see her for the best person she wants to be. To do this you have to not get too personal because when we men get personal, it's about her body and our desire to see her clothes strewn about the room. It's how we're built and there's no shame in that but we need to use it in a more productive manner so that, yes, it is more often her idea when her clothes are strewn about the room.

And here's the conundrum, by showing her we value her for more than sex, we get more sex.

I know; it just about blows the mind.

So when you are giving her a compliment, choose the subject carefully. If it is a body part, stay safe, her eyes, her smile, the tilt of her chin in the soft summer light, her eyebrows as they arch when she asks a question, the way she twists a strand of her hair when she is thinking, her lips on a crisp spring morning. All of this shows her you see her and notice her and this alone will set you apart from most other men.

Another thing you can use as a foundation of a good compliment is a shared experience. The first time you kissed her or held her hand or saw her or went to a show or played golf or whatever. By demonstrating to her that the time and experiences you have had together are an inspiration and a joy, you let her know you appreciate her.

I can see the puzzlement in your mind.

"Wait a minute, 'notice her, appreciate her,' what's next, 'pamper her?' I already did that."

Guys, when we first started I told you this whole thing had to be treated like a new hobby. I don't know about your hobbies but mine do not consist of a checklist of one-and-done things. My hobbies consume a lot of time and everything I do for my hobbies I try to use as often as possible.

It's the same thing here. We don't forget about the foundation, we use it in everything we do. So your compliments should cover the spectrum of noticing her and appreciating her and pampering her and guess what, with the "Pamper her" compliment you get to highlight something you did for her that made you feel good or brought a smile to her face or created a special moment between you both.

Recall the time her smile warmed your day after you brought her flowers or coffee or her favourite treat. Be shameless in remembering the nice things you've done for her because you are reminding her why you do them, her smile, her laugh, her warm embrace, her lips on yours, her head on your shoulder. You are reminding her and letting her know you remember all of this and that pampering her is important to you.

But I know the whole compliment thing is daunting. So this is what we are going to do; first we'll break down a typical compliment, then I will give you 52 compliments in the form of poetry.

Some of these may not exactly fit your situation and that's OK. Take the ones that do and use them. And since they are poetry, she will forgive you for them not being original. The goal at the end of a year is that you are creating your own compliments that are based around your life together and are directly inspired by her. But until you are ready for that, I have got your back.

But first, the compliment.

The eyes and smile; they are the easiest thing about her you can compliment. They are expressive and unique and non-threatening. What that means is that it must not appear as if your only goal is to get her naked. Yes, I know that is our first goal and you know that is our first goal and she knows that is our first goal and that's one of the things that becomes a problem so we're looking to show her that there is more and compliments are one way to do this.

The next thing to take into consideration is your surroundings. A good compliment should be created on the spot to highlight the inspiration of events. So take notice of your surrounding and fold them into the compliment. Take notice of lights and the sky and the architecture and anything else that can be used to make this special.

And the last thing to put into the compliment is how you are affected. If you felt content or happy or awed or whatever, let her know. This is the reaction she wants; she wants to know she affects your life in more than a "my pants are tight" manner.

So, let's take a stab at this, shall we? We'll use her eyes, a cloudy sky at night, and you feeling happy. Great, we've got all the components, but how to put it together?

Start with her, add the environment, and end with your feelings. Something akin to the following:

"I see the stars are hiding, they must be afraid to compete with the light in your eyes and the happiness in mine."

Simple, short, and something she can tell is for her.

And that is the art of the compliment. Sincere and short and created just for her. But don't be afraid to write things down at first. It will help the process and you can see what works and what does not before you tell her.

Passion Poetry and 52 Compliments

Passion poetry is not love poetry. Passion poetry focuses on moments and circumstances and does not pretend to be a unique emotion or feeling or declaration. It also should not make us cringe to read it a week later. Passion poetry is about a relationship not about describing the mythical perfect person.

Love poetry is all about pedestals and angels and other things we come to despise as the first blush of infatuation wears off and we have to actually deal with the real person underneath and have to make those decisions as to what we can stand and what sets our teeth on edge, no matter how good she looks with her clothes strewn about the room.

Most love poetry is difficult to read. It's vapid and pretentious and represents itself and its subject matter as unique. The bare fact is that everyone has loved. Everyone has had that feeling of yearning in their chest. Everyone has been so distracted by the habits and appearance of another that they are driven to overlook any flaw in character; right up until you hate them for it.

Passion poetry removes itself from that environment and is more concerned with the circumstances of why you are in a relationship. It is the mundane moments, the chance encounters and comforting memories. This is what keeps passion alive in a relationship. Lust is wonderful but passion can be forever.

And guys, women like you to tell them why you love them. They like you to tell them why moments are special. They love to hear that just their smile affected your day.

So I'm going to give you 52 passion poems in the Compliment form. They are short, just six lines, and they cover a range of subjects and can be used as an apology or a greeting or a reminder that you are not a complete and utter moron, no matter what else you may do to cement that concept in her mind.

The goal is for you to pen something yourself. Until you are ready, use these.

As for the Compliment form of poetry, this explanation is for those who wonder about poetry structure. If that is not you, ignore it, it will have no effect on you or your relationship, and skip straight to the poems on the next pages.

The Compliment form is a short form structured to capture and produce passion poetry in a manageable size and presentation. An epic poem of hundreds of lines is a difficult thing to read and nearly impossible to share. But six lines on why a day was special or how a smile warmed you or how a kiss gave you comfort, that is manageable and can be shared.

So the Compliment form consists of a title and six lines. The title is integral to the poem. It should set the mood or start the question or posit the circumstance. The first five lines should expand on the emotional content of the story and the last line should resolve and enhance the conclusion.

The Compliment form uses blank style verse (metered but no rhyming) and the structure of the lines is as follows:

There is a trimeter (six syllables) title, five lines of tetrameter (eight syllables), and trimeter end line. The declining meter of line six adds a natural ending to the form and bookends the title structure.

I am providing you 52 Compliment poems and a suggestion that you hand write one on a card or note and give it to her once a week. And yes, this means you had a solid year of compliments to give her. Some of them even cover getting angry and how you respond and some are outright apologies. It's like I've been there.

If you can take what we've discussed and use these as examples to construct your own, please do so. She won't mind you hand copying something for her but she would prefer if you created it instead. And when you do, tell her you did.

It would be like you were noticing her and appreciating her and pampering her, because you are.

What a concept.

A Brief Moment in Time

We laughed together, hands entwined,

and I longed to bend and kiss you

but stopped to drink your happiness

and let it fill me with content

like joy and peace and paradise;

while waiting were your lips.

An Accidental Smile

I did not perfectly realise

the peril as that first stray smile

broke on me like inspiration

and set my guarded heart reeling

and stirred within my weary soul

a hope for happiness.

As We Gathered with Friends

I was happy for the soft lights

and the noise and the distractions

as I glanced in your direction

because no one saw me sighing

as I longed to stand next to you

and bend and kiss your lips.

At Eleanor's On Main

We were sitting over coffee

while you told me about your day

and the trials and the triumphs

of randomly odd frustrations

and I took your hand happily

in that sidewalk cafe.

Between Two Hurried Steps

Today I found my thoughts turning

to you and your smile and the way

your eyes sparkle before you laugh

and I stopped to catch my breath

and in this happy reflection

I longed to hold you close.

Dreams Dreamt From a Distance

I watched today as the setting sun

lit your face and burnished your hair

and as you turned to face the warmth

a smile played across your lips

and I dreamed that your happiness

included thoughts of me.

I Gave a Gentle Sigh

It was a Thursday of a week

that had been filled with little more

than continuous disaster

that strived to wear me down and then

I remembered when we first kissed,

and everything was well.

I Remember a Glance

I caught your eye from a distance

and my heart stuttered at your smile

and as we chatted through the crowd

my pulse quickened with each footstep

until eternity faded

and I could hold you close.

I Was Captivated

You'd fallen asleep on the couch

as the evening wandered away

and as I sat there next to you

and softly breathed in your perfume

I reached out and caressed your hair

and you smiled in your sleep.

Imagining Autumn

With the city sounds around me,

I stood silent at the corner,

anxious with anticipation,

as I longed for the sight of you.

Suddenly a sound of running

And you were in my arms.

In The Space Between Words

When last we talked, I longed that time

would fail for all eternity

so that those bright, fleeting, seconds,

Those wry moments of happiness,

might be reflected forever

like passion in your eyes.

It Was 3:52

There was a rare quiet moment

In a day choked with dissonance;

I thought of you and warmly smiled

because I knew this day would end

and we would share a cup of tea

and a soft, yearning kiss.

Near Sunrise and Passion

It was a Tuesday in April

and the Spring sun was new and bright

and the morning breeze trod crisply

over the freshly thawed landscape

while my mind wandered carelessly;

until I spotted you.

Once Passion Slipped My Mind

It was a day filled with shopping

and as we strolled from store to store

my patience began to wither

and my mood began to tatter;

then you hugged me and kissed my neck

and, oh, I remembered.

One Day in November

The weather was miserable

and the cold wind promised nothing

except a melancholy rain

and then your smile came to mind

the lips, the eyes, the attitude

and I found comfort there.

One Pleasant Day in June

There was a breeze that touched your cheek

and captured a wisp of your hair.

And as it draped across your neck

your hand gently caressed it while

a smile played across your lips

and I envied that breeze.

One Sunday Afternoon

On a day of no consequence

as we wandered about the house,

straightening this and cleaning that

you paused and took me by the hand

and softly whispered you loved me;

it brought tears to my eyes.

The First Hour I Loved You

We were standing apart that day

chatting with various people

about unimportant subjects

when I looked up and caught your eye

and we shared an indulgent smile

and promises of joy.

The First Time I Kissed You

There are those who just remember

the time, the place, the circumstance

of that soft touch of eager lips

but in my mind is so much more

as anxious anticipation

became a life with you.

The Quiet in My Soul

I always have the ready words

and clever quip on guileless tongue

to give a pause, compel a smile,

and bring a tear to doubtful eye,

but when near you, I am silent;

you take my breath away.

The Reflections You Bring

There's not a pedestal around

that you'd agree to occupy;

your passion seeps into the world

like a flood of raw circumstance;

perhaps that's why I came to love

the time I spend with you.

There Amid The Clamour

We stood together in a room;

the noise, the crowd, the distractions,

and within all the confusion,

amongst all the cunning discord,

you brushed your fingers over mine

and smiled a blissful smile.

Tuesday, After Dinner

We stood calmly washing dishes,

by chance it was your turn to dry,

And every time you took a dish

you caressed my hand so slightly

by the time the sink was empty,

my heart was full of you.

Upon the Day's First Light

I woke today to quiet thoughts

of the fleeting time we spend close

and of the time we spend apart

and as I longed to comfort you

and imagined you in my arms,

my thoughts comforted me.

Where Once an Empty Sky

Your beauty breaks upon the day

like a sensual winter's sun,

like a kaleidoscope of hope,

like a passionate thunderbolt,

searing an enticing image

within my warming soul.

Within a Cautious Glance

There was that uncertain instant

when first I held your hand in mine

and pondered if I could make known

how I coveted this moment,

and as I raised my eyes to yours;

I sighed and was content.

You Made Me Laugh That Day

We'd been in the car for hours

when you quietly sighed and said

"Please, I need you to pull over,"

and when the car was at a stop

you softly kissed me on the lips,

then thumped me on the nose.

Arguments I Once Had

I have always loudly declared

that love at first sight is fiction;

that it is mere self-deception

the desperate mind plays on our heart

and those who embrace it are fools;

then one day I saw you.

Discarding Resentment

We had stopped at the grocery store

to pick up the things for dinner

and, as usual, you wandered

until minutes became an hour

but as my temper was fraying,

you kissed me a "sorry."

On Thoughts Best Left Unsaid

There are times you make me angry

and I wonder how an adult

could behave in such a manner

but before words leap from my mouth

I remind myself I love you

and know you love me too.

One Evening after Work

As we stood in that stagnant line

and listened to squabbling

of those who steadfastly refused

to see the joy and happiness

in the lives they built together,

we laughed and shared a kiss.

Reflections One Midnight

I stopped looking for perfection

but never stopped looking for love

in the ordinary moments

of a life lived in the knowledge

that passion is no accident;

which is why I love you.

While We Were Out Walking

The snow was lighting in your hair

in the soft glow of the evening

as the crisp wind danced around you

until I could not plainly tell

where reality ended and

my dreams of you began.

The Ordinary Cure

An ordinary sunrise crept

upon an ordinary day

and filled the ordinary lives

of the ordinary people

with all the ordinary things,

for no one else had you.

One Fine Spring Afternoon

We were caught by a sudden storm

that announced itself with thunder,

with hailstones from an empty sky,

with rain so cold our lips turned blue.

You looked at me and laughed and said

"The weatherman was wrong."

In the Early Moonlight

As dusk gathered around our feet

a seductive moon softly teased

up the darkening horizon

wandering through the garnet sky

whispering ardent prophecy

of a future with you.

Decisions I Have Made

The morning sun crept gingerly

as if, perhaps, it was afraid

that it had crassly intruded

upon fragile circumstances,

but I laughed and kissed you lightly

as I lay next to you.

At Work One Afternoon

When I called to pose a question

your tone told me the day was bad

and my random interruption

did nothing to make it better

so I brought flowers home for you

and asked to rub your feet.

Anger is a Poor Choice

We were mad at each other

over something we were convinced

was worth the temper and shouting

and the hurt we desired to cause,

so I told you that I loved you

because words can't be unsaid.

As We Sat Over Drinks

I thought about being jealous

but then realised it would not help

because you define elegance

and that other men notice you

only declares they saw too late

what I loved from the first.

Inspiration Recalled

In my mind I keep a picture

of the first time I saw you smile

because I had entered the room

and how it made my heart stutter;

it makes me yearn to kiss your lips

and hold you close to me.

On The Way Home from Work

I had decided not to cook

so stopped at my favourite diner

to clear my head and organise

for a softly cluttered evening

when I saw you sitting alone

and had to know your name.

I Wanted to Tell You

I love your eyes, your laugh, your smile,

the way the sunlight strikes your hair,

the soft feel of your hand in mine,

but what I love most about you

is the way you can forgive me

when I have been stupid.

One January Morn

As I looked out onto the world

covered in Winter's hoary dross,

I considered all the heartache

that schemed to fill each empty day,

and reveled that I had found you

to hold in grateful arms.

I Forget To Exhale

Like a soft breeze you drifted in

and suddenly I was breathless

as the room came into focus

around you and that stunning smile;

I am no longer surprised that

this happens every time.

Solace in Memory

I keep a favourite photograph

in my wallet and phone and mind

of you laughing in the sunlight

in the joy of the patient day

and when my life is troublesome

your smile, it comforts me.

Why I Love Films with You

As we waited for the movie

in a half empty theatre

and watched the previews one by one

you softly whispered appraisals

of "Yes," "Rental," or "Dear God no"

and each time nipped my ear.

I Saw the Sky Blushing

As the sun slipped into the clouds

and then beneath the horizon

the world was filled with emotion

and the heavens wept violet tears

as the day hid from your beauty

and I was not surprised.

As I Enter the Room

I love when you first notice me,

the happiness that lights your eyes

the smile appearing on your face

and I am counting the seconds

before your lips gladly touch mine

as my heart skips a beat.

As We Washed the Dishes

After dinner one quiet night

we were talking in the kitchen

about our days and random things

and as I handed you a dish

you caressed my hand and softly

told me that you loved me.

On Silly Holidays

I must admit I am amused

by gentlemen who once a year

pretend and falsify romance

with the same thoughtless concoctions

instead of investing their life

with passion, love, and you.

Methods in My Madness

I could walk with you forever

or at least until your feet hurt

just so that I might have the chance

to bring that smile to your lips

as I massage the tiredness

and replace it with me.

Last Words

Guys, most of what I've put in here are common sense things. You can tell they are common sense things by the way they are so often ignored, like changing the batteries in your smoke alarms or turning off the breaker before you repair a socket or turning off the mower before you clear the output chute.

Or taking a wonderful woman for granted.

Or letting yourself be taken advantage of, for that matter.

We all get caught up in our lives and the things we consider solved we ignore. Just so you know; a relationship is never solved. If you put a fraction of the time you do into your other hobbies into maintaining a relationship, you will be amazed at the result. And just so we are clear, I consider hobbies to be nearly sacrosanct. I put a lot of time into mine because they are important to me, aid me in some manner, make me feel better about myself, and are fun even if I am occasionally red faced from screaming and so angry I want to spit nails.

Sound familiar? It should, it applies to both hobbies and relationships.

We, as men, have to get past what other men think of our relationships. When you find that woman who is the right brand of crazy and who is attracted to you, why the hell would you let your friends dissuade you from happiness?

So the theme here is that the only person you need to convince is that woman you love. If love is too strong a word for you, call her that woman who you can't wait to see and hold and be near. If she is good with you, everyone else can go pound sand.

But, and this is critical, if you have to participate in being treated poorly, run, because she is not the right brand of crazy. She's just a manipulative shrew looking to leech the worth from your soul while disparaging you to all and seeking another victim. If you have to change for her rather than are inspired to change because of her, run. If compromise means always doing it her way, run. If you find yourself saying, "but she's a really great person," to people all the time, run.

And if she asks you to give up your hobbies, the first one you give up is her.

Oh, and if you are the one doing all the demanding, doing all the posturing, doing all the disparaging, she deserves better than you.

But if you are willing to grow and mature in order to be the man she deserves, make certain she deserves you. The only thing worse than a relationship ending is it continuing on inertia until resentment and hatred are the only things either of you feel.

And remember these two critical items.

1. Men are children, women are insane

2. There are important things, there are unimportant things, choose carefully.

Because as always, it's not about being right, it's about being happy.

I've said it before; I'm repeating it because it's important.

About the Author

Born in 1961 into an enlisted Navy family of an eventual five boys, Jonathan grew up on or around military bases, doing all the normal things boys in the 1960's and 1970's did. A writer from an early age, Jonathan has published three volumes of poetry, is publishing a book of short stories in early 2011, has written for numerous websites, is a writing mentor in on-line workshops, and fills his time with work and hobbies.

Jonathan's relationship advice is born of experience. He has twice been married and twice been a custodial single parent. His foray into dating after each marriage ended taught him many things, most importantly that woman are indeed insane and fighting it is like fighting the need for breathing. You can do it but the results are catastrophic.

Jonathan currently lives in the Philadelphia, Pennsylvania area with his youngest son, Gareth, his rescue mutt, Lady, and three cats that also were left behind when his second marriage ended and spends his time writing, teaching and training in martial arts, making armour for and participating in SCA heavy combat, making props for and performing with the We Are Street Circus troupe, playing video and other games, and waiting for Sandra Bullock to come to her senses and call him.

It's not a great plan, but it hasn't failed entirely; yet.

He hasn't sworn off relationships, he's just not willing to endure the wrong brand of crazy a third time.